# THE MODEL INMATE

## MIND OVER MATTER: HOW I BECAME THE MODEL INMATE

## RA'SUN ALLAH

FAMS

FREE ALL MY SONS

**For further information, please contact**:
Free All My Suns, Inc.
Raleigh, NC
www.freeallmysuns.org


OR


S.U.N. Publishing, LLC
P.O. Box #3624
New Haven, Connecticut 06515
Visit our website at: www.rasunallah.com


Written by I-Noble Ra'Sun Allah
Printed in the United States of America

*Dedicated to my wife, Jacqueline Marie Allah...*
*The one who inspired me to write this book and who continues*
*on a daily basis to inspire me to see my full potential in life and*
*not limit myself.*

# CONTENTS

# INTRODUCTION

Many have been led to believe or just out right believe that when one becomes incarcerated and labeled an inmate, there exists this magic switch that one can just flick and automatically turn off all the criminal thoughts and behaviors that has brought one to prison in the first place. Well, let me be the first to inform you that this just isn't so! Because just as Rome wasn't built in one day or night, you cannot expect to see a change manifest itself in a man as soon as he finds himself incarcerated.

So, what I am striving to convey to the readers of this book is the many trials and tribulations I found myself faced with when I got locked-up and became inmate #193919. My hope is that these experiences can assist you along your personal journey towards becoming *The Model Inmate.*

It has been said that "*the model inmate is the inmate who just hasn't been caught in a while.*" Well, for the purpose of this book, the model inmate here is defined as any inmate/prisoner/convict/lil' homie/big homie/comrade, etc. who has made the conscious decision to be someone as well as something better than who and what they were before they found themselves on lockdown.

Will this be easy? Emphatically NO! It will most certainly take a level of commitment and discipline on ones' part to do so. I know because my personal journey was not one that was met with ease...So, please read along these lines and feel my pain, my joys, my ups', my downs and ultimately what it took for me to become the model inmate.

1

# REMOVED FROM THE STREETS

Wednesday August 26, 1992 I was scheduled to appear in court for the numerous criminal cases that I had accumulated over the years since I was charged with murder. Yeah! One would think that after being charged with murder I would sit my ass down and chill out; at least until I saw what the outcome of those serious charges I was faced with would be. But I was in those streets head first and by any means necessary!

*"However, unbeknownst to me a warrant was issued for my arrest for some shit I had did several weeks prior. See, me and two friends of mine at the time were out at the Cats Club and the Cats Club was the biggest thing to happen in New Haven in a long time as far as the club scene was concerned. So, while at the club I crossed paths with an off duty police officer who patrolled my neighborhood. This night in particular the club was live, the ladies were everywhere, and I had some of my boys with me. The vibes were right and everyone was in a good mood; especially me, due to the fact that I was underage and was able to buy my way into the festivities on this night. I held a corner in the club and was purchasing endless rounds of drinks for those within my circumference. This officer had the opportunity of*

*witnessing just how much love I was getting from the women that he could only admire from afar. As I looked in his direction I could clearly see the discontent written all over his face. So, I gave him a nod of the head and a wave with a fist full oh 20s, 50s, and 100s.*

*However, before I had gotten to the Cats Club that night, my day was like any other day out on Congress Avenue with my crew. Daily we sold a shit load of drugs accompanied by a lot of drinking, and smoking endless Philly Blunts of Buddha (weed) laced with Crazy Eddie (PCP) angel dust. At this time, I had one of the biggest dust spots in the neighborhood. It was nothing for me to get into my car and drive the hour ride south to New York on I-95 until I reached Harlem and get off at the 138<sup>th</sup> Street exit, cross the bridge, make a left at the light, then a right and ride along the railway on Park Avenue until I got to the Crazy Eddie spot. I made this trip daily to 116<sup>th</sup> Street and Park Avenue in Harlem to spend at least seven or eight thousand on Crazy Eddie. Bags of dust went for $10 in Harlem; however, once I trafficked them across state lines and into the city of New Haven, each bag went for 20 bills a pop easily! Almost everybody in the city that smoked dust hustled so you didn't have to take any shorts unless you were giving someone a deal and because I was purchasing so many bags at one time I was able to get a three-dollar discount on each one. I was only paying just $7 a bag.*

*The money I was making from the sale of dust worked for me. Also, because We prided ourselves on smoking the best shit out during this time, it was nothing for dudes from around my way to take that drive from New Haven to 113<sup>th</sup> and Lenox Avenue to the Nucleus or 133<sup>rd</sup> and Amsterdam Avenue to the Patty Shack and cop several hundred bags of Buddha... When they saw those Connecticut tags roll up on the scene they knew that we were there to spend a few grand.*

*Anyway after the club had let out, I was in the mood to smoke something; but I needed some Philly blunts so I drove my car* *over to the corner of Whalley and Sherman Avenue to the local 24-hour store. Low and behold I would find myself coming face-to-face with this joker who was off duty and hanging out at the Cats Club. It was obvious he was getting ready to act up because he had too many drinks. As I stood in line before the cashier to pay for the items I intended on purchasing this jackass goes and sits his items down on the counter along with mines and had the nerve to order me to pay for them. This left me boiling inside and by the time I returned to the car I was vexed! I mean steaming mad! So, I waited for him to come out of the store and get into his ride and I proceeded to chase him all throughout New Haven that night. Trust me when I tell you, god was on his side because had I caught his ass that night there would have been one less officer on the New Haven police force. (**I'm glad that I am telling this story minus the charge of killing a police officer.**) Shortly after the chase begun he drove over to the Yale police station near the New Haven Green to seek refuge in the arms of the campus police. I would be locked up that night for a number of traffic violations associated with the chase. However, I did not think that weeks later this officer would seek stiffer charges against me because he was literally in fear for his life after the nights' events.*"

On the morning of August 26, 1992 the New Haven Superior Court would receive a bomb threat. The court house would be evacuated and searched. I and others were instructed to return back to court after the 12 o'clock recess. Upon returning all court hearings for the day had been postpone to a later date. So, I left the court house and got into my car and started to drive in the direction of the Fair Haven section of town. As I drove up Hamilton Street towards Grand Avenue, I went to make a right onto Grand Avenue. Just as I approached the light, I looked to the right and I saw that the lanes were blocked in both directions with Officers standing in front of their patrol car doors with guns drawn on me; so, my quick reflexes told me to turn left in an attempt to get away from them. Then as I looked to my left I could see the same thing taking place! There were two patrol cars facing me and blocking the road in both directions. *Yeah! Even with my license I considered myself a runner...* So, as I peered into the rearview mirror I could see what looked like a dozen marked and unmarked cars behind me. Damn, I was caught!!! I put my hands through the sunroof to surrender before I was pulled from my car in the middle of the street and thrust into the back seat of an unmarked car and driven to the police headquarters at One Union Avenue.

I was brought into the booking area where I was told to take off all of my clothing for a strip search. The strip search is by and far the most emasculating thing that any man has to bear. You are in an area where Police Officers and Correction Officers come and go as they please. While you are being instructed to take off your belongings one at a time and hand them over to the Correction Officer to inspect for contraband. Imagine standing in front of a man butt ass naked as he runs his hands through your drawers to make sure you haven't hidden anything in them. Or imagine being told by this same man to bend over at your waist and spread your butt cheeks so that he can examine your ass for hidden jewels! Or being ordered to lift your nut sack, then run those same fingers through your mouth and lift your tongue. This shit is degrading. So, after experiencing this trauma, I was taken to a holding cell.

Word to everything I love, I could not take the sight nor smell of this area. The toilet looked as if it had never been cleaned since the building was first built with a permanent ring of shit around the bowl. There was spit all over the walls. Even the floors and the benches made me cringe from the filth that lay on top of them. I didn't even want to touch the bars. So, I had chosen to stand for as long as I possibly could and I was tired as hell by the time I was moved to the back where the other holding cells were.

Having no idea why I was being detained at this particular time, I sat cool, calm and collected until I was escorted up to the investigative unit where Assistant Chief Warren sat waiting to berate me for chasing his officer at 5am in the morning. He had mentioned to me how he was tired of the terror that was being put in on the streets of New Haven and how he and the feds were now choosing to handle the situation starting with the Jungle Boys...whom I was closely associated with at this time. The F.B.I., along with State and Local Police had acted out raids on The Jungle Boys on June 21, 1992 and pretty much dismantled their entire operation.

Early on during my incarceration when I had started ordering and reading books regularly I remember vividly the night I was laying on my bunk reading the book "African American Organized Crime, by Rufus Schatzberg & Robert J. Kelly" when I came across an excerpt in there about the Jungle that read:

*"The example of the "Jungle Boys," a former African American New Haven, Connecticut gang, illustrates the trend toward entrepreneurial, organized criminality occurring within some youth gangs.*

*Formed in 1984, they were linked early on with drug trafficking in New Haven. The gang established a command hierarchy resembling, and possibly emulating, the power structure of a Cosa Nostra crime family, with a boss, underboss, lieutenants, and soldiers. Before they were dismantled, the Jungle Boys had virtually taken over a housing complex and intimidated the local neighborhood residents and businesses for more than five years.*

*In 1992, a law enforcement task force composed of Federal Bureau of Investigation, Drug Enforcement Administration, Alcohol, Tobacco, and firearms (Department of treasury), and State and local police, raided gang locales, arrested the leadership, charged them with drug offenses under RICO statutes and destroyed the gangs.*

*In this case, the traditional characteristics of street gangs—*

*defense of territory, recreational use of illegal substances, and petty crime—were not the defining features of the gang's identity: The Jungle Boys did not mobilize to protect their geographical locales---although based in a metropolitan area. In fact, many of the members lived outside the city and engaged in the purchase and sale of real estate for investment purposes. The gang's durability and strength (it required a Task Force of federal, state and municipal law enforcement agencies to mount a meaningful response to it) depended not solely on its reputation for violence and coercion but on its capacity to integrate itself into the legitimate segments of the local community by defining itself publicly as a "Cultural organization," by sponsoring "community meetings," with local business professionals, by applying for city grants and development money while engaging in extortion and gun play with other gang rivals. In all of this it was frightfully effective.*

*As the Jungle Boys and other groups demonstrate, gang recruitment processes are not limited to street and neighborhood assessments of prospective members, but are facilitated through the large and dangerous prison system. Strong ties formed in street gangs are sustained even in prison, and rather than suppress gang activity, prisons tend to perpetuate it, and because the gangs are so influential in the prison, as they are in many neighborhoods, inmates feel compelled to affiliate with one gang or another to survive the incarceration experience.*

*Outside, in the communities and neighborhoods, gangs such as the Jungle Boys and its Hispanic equivalent, the powerful Latin Kings, spread across the archipelago of impoverished neighborhoods, transforming them, redefining their social geography into "set," gang terrains, that are defended because they function as criminal markets for the gangster/businessman..."*

The Assistant Chief was steaming mad that while I had been out on 1.3 million dollars in bonds, and given several chances at my freedom, I was still wreaking havoc on the streets. So in his anger, he informed me that my bond was being set at One million dollars and he dared me to make that. Let's just say a lot was going on with the family where the feds were on our heels at this time or I would have posted that bond just to rub it in that fuckers face.

So, this was indeed my last day on the streets of New Haven. Over 28 years later and I still haven't returned yet! Just something to think about before you get into the streets head first or if you are behind these prison walls with me simply ask yourself, was it at all worth it? Also, this is just one of the many trials and tribulations that I would face on my journey towards becoming the model inmate.

### *My thoughts*

 As I look back on my life now I often wonder what could I have done different now that I did not do back then? I mean look at me and as you continue to read you will see exactly what my life has become. I am sitting in front of a computer typing this story which is my third book. So, there should be no doubt in my mind or anyone else's for that matter that I could have been a writer early on if I had just applied myself. Also, I didn't have to wait until I was twenty-years into my sentence to pen my first work. I guess the message that I am striving to convey is if you are incarcerated and reading this book, don't waste a moment of your time figuring out what it is that you want to do with the rest of your life because the time is now! If you are physically free use the words on these pages to free yourself mentally so that you don't have to be faced with the suffering that myself and so many others incarcerated have to deal with. Seek to find your potential on the outside and don't ever put yourself in the position where it takes you being locked away in a cage to know exactly who you are!"

*I have only just a minute.*
*Only sixty seconds in it.*
*Forced upon me, can't refuse it.*
*Didn't seek it, didn't choose it.*
*But it's up to me to use it.*
*I must suffer if I lose it.*
*Give account if I abuse it,*
*Just a tiny little minute but eternity is in it.*
*- Benjamin E. Mays*

# 2

## DAY ONE

Once taken into custody, I was processed into the city lockup and place in a cell where I would remain until I would be taken over to the court house on Elm Street to be arraigned on these new charges the next morning. As I sat in the cell, I saw the bail bondsmen who had informed me that my bond was set at one million dollars. When I arrived at the court house, I went upstairs to stand before the judge only to have my bail raised from one million to 1.5 million dollars. Before the hour struck five o'clock, I found myself back in the cell rubbing my head wondering and thinking what the hell have I just done to my life and about all of the things that I left behind on the streets. My family, my baby's mother was just three months pregnant with my child and those who I once knew as friends who would now be looking for friendships in someone else to replace me. Beans said it best when he rapped "You got five years in never flown a kite, hearing grown men moan at night…" I ain't been flown a kite because the niggas that I ran with couldn't read or write. Now I'm locked up with car notes, rent, bills, drugs, money and all of my other worldly possessions that would now be left behind in the hands of someone that I would have to "trust."

I spent more than three weeks over on the Union Avenue lockup; at One Union Avenue, which is located on the lower level of the New Haven Police Department. The average stay over there is about a week; or so, if you are unable to make bond. However, since my bond was now set at 1.5 million dollars; and my status was now elevated to one of high security, I was told that I could not be transferred over to the county jail on Whalley Avenue at night when all the other transfers are regularly done. Therefore, I was being informed that my move would be taking place during the daylight hours. These assholes thought someone might try to break me out! SMH!

When I arrived at the Whalley Avenue county jail my first day, I found myself entering into a culture that no man should ever have to experience. The Whalley Avenue county jail was the place where the small city police departments within the New Haven County would send those who could not post bail. New arrivals came there every day from New Haven, Meriden, Waterbury, and other small urban and suburban enclaves. First, I would be placed into a large holding cell that I and other first timers would come to know simply as "the bullpen." Most of these men held in the bullpen had such foul odors from not washing for several days or even weeks. The stench that came off of their bodies while standing in close proximity to them literally made me sick to my stomach! One at a time a tall white Corrections Officer named "6-9" (No! I'm not talking about Tekashi69... smile!) would pull us from the bullpen, sit us at a chair on the side of his desk and ask us a series of questions like "what's your name", "what's your date of birth", "what's your address" etc. Once I was taken through this method, I was taken over to a wall where I was asked to stand with my back to the wall and face the camera. Several pictures were taken of me in different poses, I was told to face the camera and then told to turn to my right side and then to my left side and those three photos or mug shots of me were placed into what I would come to know as a master file. This is the same time inmate number 193919 was assigned to me. I was no longer Ray V. Boyd; but, just a number.

Once this was complete I was then escorted back into the bullpen where I would sit and wait for another three hours. This waiting game was something that was played out on a regular basis. I sense that it was by design to break you down mentally because everyone in the bullpen would be tired and fatigued by the time we were moved into the next phase of this intake process.

Next another Correction Officer would come and call you by your number "Inmate 1-9-3-9-1-9!" and your name "BOYD!" this would draw attention to you from all onlookers who were being nosey as all hell because they knew about your case. I would step up to the entrance of the bullpen and wait for the C.O. to open the gate and proceed to follow him to a back room area where there were several showers, stacks of white towels, shower shoes, pieces of soap, and this strange quill shampoo that everyone entering the facility had to bath in to remove crabs and lice from their body. Once you stripped down, your clothing would be taken by one of the inmates who worked in the A.P. room and placed in a black traveling bags and stored it away for your next court appearance.

After I had jumped into the shower, I lathered my body in the disinfectant shampoo, washed, rinsed off, and then stepped out of the shower to dry my entire body off with a towel the size of a face cloth. Not to mention how I had to put back on the same soiled boxer shorts that I had just taken off. The Correction Officer ordered me to go over and grab these old tan pants that lay neatly on top of a table awaiting me. Only god knows how many men were told to put on these exact same pants before I had to wear them!

For some strange reason as I got closer to the table there was this strong chemical smell that permeated the air. It smelt like someone had left the stove on and gas was leaking throughout the building. I had no idea where it was coming from but it was starting to give me a serious fucking headache. The inmate worker handed me three t-shirts and another pair of pants that were stamped with the letters NHCC; which stood for 'New Haven Correctional Center', on them. Also, I was given two old white (filthy) sheets, a wool blanket that no one would use to sleep under because this shit would make you itch all night, a state towel, and a mesh laundry bag.

Once I had grabbed up the laundry bag, an officer had escorted me and several others to the housing units where we had been assigned a cell. Remind you, I started hustling at the age of twelve, never lived in the projects and in my mind's eye I never experienced poverty on any level until I walked through the door way of this two-man cell! But, trust and believe I come from poverty on all levels! As I entered the cell my first sight was what use to be a stainless steel toilet that now looked as if it had not been cleaned in years. Then there was this old man who stood and extended his wrinkled hand to greet me. I had no idea who this complete stranger was; so, I just gave him a head nod. I am sure that he could identify with my frustration of being in this cage when I was just a free man several weeks' ago; because, he gave back a nod before lowering his hand.

I threw the laundry bag on the top of this nasty ass soiled mattress and just sat at the desk holding my head. The mattress had all kinds of stains up and down its entire surface. It looked like a combination of slobber from some heavy sleeper drooling all damn night. Some urine stains possibly from some grown ass man who could not hold his piss at night, or some frighten man-child who was just too afraid to get off of his bunk that night. It looked and smelt like an addict had literally took a shit on it as he was going through withdrawals from either alcohol or heroin. Some stains I am now sure came from the perverted individual who masturbated and decided that he was just going to sleep in his semen that night. Hell! I could not tell what it was, I just knew that this night, my grown ass had to lay down in it! (Laugh! -Now cry for me!).

Several hours later I had to make the sacrifice of laying in this shit. So, I stood up onto the chair, threw the sheets over top of the mattress and took my black ass to bed.

### *My thoughts*

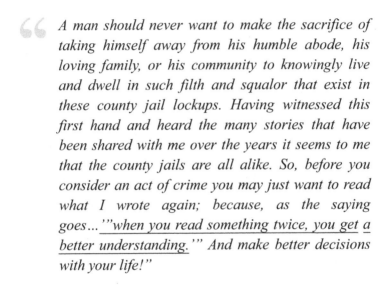 *A man should never want to make the sacrifice of taking himself away from his humble abode, his loving family, or his community to knowingly live and dwell in such filth and squalor that exist in these county jail lockups. Having witnessed this first hand and heard the many stories that have been shared with me over the years it seems to me that the county jails are all alike. So, before you consider an act of crime you may just want to read what I wrote again; because, as the saying goes…'"when you read something twice, you get a better understanding.'" And make better decisions with your life!"*

# 3

## CHOW CALL

While I was at the lock up on Union Avenue, I found it hard to eat the food they were serving us down there for the life of me. I could not stomach the food. The food would arrive in the back of a suburban truck where the trays were stacked on top of the other about six high with a belt that held them in their place. Once the belt was removed you could see the condensation running off the trays as if it were a leaking faucet. Because there were no tables or chairs in these holding cells there was no options other than sitting the tray on your lap or holding it with one hand as you ate with the other hand. The food was some shit that you have never seen before in your life I can guarantee you of that! And it was something that I would never feed my dog… However, they knew someone would eventually eat it if they got hungry enough.

It was the responsibility of one or more of the trusted inmates who work at this location to handle and pass out the food trays to us. They would even drive over to the county jail with the Correction Officers to pick up the food. For reasons unbeknownst to me they had inmates that lived and worked at this site. I would later come to learn that many of these men were either on their ways home and their risk levels low; so, they met all the safety criteria to stay there. Some even were given outside clearance status where they were more than willing to risk their freedom by introducing contraband into the lockup that sat on the lower level of the police station!

This is the first time I had experienced someone being given preferential treatment for the crime they had committed. There was this older fella in the lockup that everyone seemed to revere for some reason or another. He was never called by an inmate number; but, by his name...Mr. Perkins!

I had come to learn that Mr. Perkins, had murdered his wife and would later plead guilty to a lesser charge than murder. Therefore, this allowed for him to serve his sentence at the Union Avenue lockup. This information had resonated with me because I knew of him and heard about his case. His case had sent shockwaves through the City of New Haven. Hell! He owned the biggest funeral home in the City during this time that catered to performing the home going services for just about two-thirds of the blacks who passed away. He was respectful and very polite; but, he took his wife's life for Christ sake! But, I'm not mad at him; shit, he got all the justice that his money could BUY!

Well if the aforementioned about the food in the lockup on Union Avenue left a bad taste in your mouth, let me tell you how it was when I got to the county jail for the first time.

Arriving at "Whalley"; which is the name that those associated with the criminal elements have come to call the New Haven Correctional Center, is a day that I will never forget. See, I am not a breakfast person at all so, I slept through breakfast my first morning at Whalley Avenue and by the time lunch would be coming I was hungry. I mean you should see the portion sizes that a grown man is fed at this place. The Connecticut Department of Correction is to provide the average inmate with a twenty-seven hundred calorie diet each day. Which means that every day the three meals that I was to receive had to be divided by three. So, each of my meals were to consist of 900 calories. On the street I would eat 2700 calories at the local corner store. Now, my focus was on lunch and dinner as well as how I would make it through the night on an empty stomach.

The old man had called out to me to say that lunch would be coming in a few minutes. So, I hopped down off the bunk, strolled over to the sink with a toilet attached to it to brush my teeth and wash my face before stepping out of the cell to enter into the dayroom area. Let me be the first to say that this is not a common practice by most of the inmates in the county jails. Brushing their teeth seems to be the last thing on their minds and for the life of me I could not understand why a grown ass man felt as though it was fine to approach me or any other man knowing damn well he hadn't brushed his funky ass mouth! A grown man's breath should never smell like a baby threw up in his mouth and it just sat there and rotted for a week. SMH!

Once I had walked into the day room to await lunch, there was about fifteen other individuals hanging around the television watching the Price-Is-Right or something as we waited. As soon as I saw the Tier man jump and scurry out of the way, I also got a look at two mice playing chase as they jumped out of the same elevator port where the food cart sat with cheeseburgers on it. This shit had immediately fucked with my mind which in turn fucked with my stomach and ultimately ruined my lunch for the day. I began to wonder to myself would I be strong enough to eat my dinner if I witnessed the same thing again.

Lucky for me word had got around the jail that I was there and several of my associates who had a foot hold on the movement down there at this time so they put together two bags of commissary that they felt would hold me until I was able to go to the store (commissary) for myself and get the things that I needed to see me through. This day I made a beef roman noodle soup using the warm water from the slop sink in a foul smelling closet – yeah envision that! Once I put the water in my soup and sat it down to swell (cook), I switched on the cold water in this same slop sink because I was told that the water in there got colder than the sink water in the cells. I made a nice plastic cup of grape Kool-Aid, poured a bowl of chips to eat along with my soup and tried as hard as I could to get the images of those mice playing around the food out of my head so that I could make the attempt at eating dinner.

My experience at the county jails would prove to be a bit different then when I arrived at the Cheshire Correctional Institute in the winter of 1992. I had gotten into the prison roughly around 3:30am that morning and as soon as I laid my things down on my bunk the tiers were beginning to be called for breakfast. Being the new arrival, I decided to take the long walk down the main hallway to the chow hall as a way to formularize myself with the prison and see who I could see. No matter what prison you go to in whatever state you are from, you are bound to run into someone from around your way. So, I follow the crowd as they assembled in the hall in small clusters on their way to chow. For some reason the prison dining hall has been renamed a chow hall as if this is a place where animal go to be fed.

As I entered the chow hall I followed the lead of the man before me and he took a left and then a right and grabbed his tray and took another right heading towards the back of the dining area. Since we were the first to get to the back sitting area I chose to sit at the second table just inside the doorway. I placed my tray down, took a seat and this Spanish brother approached me and stated to me "Yo! Pa' this is my table we--- sit here!" In my head this shit is eating me alive inside because all I keep telling myself is "This Motherfucker is trying to play me!!!" on my first day and "He's going to lose because I am not going nowhere- FUCK'EM! So, I stand up to square off to this jack ass and just as I positioned myself one of the kids from the jungle boys walks through the doorway and tells me to come sit with him and some other dudes that I know from the town. I got up to leave the table with my eyes locked on this Spanish cat; who I would later learn was a high ranking Latin king gang member, and as I bent the corner I'd come into contact with at least fifteen guys from all over New Haven. They showed me a lot of love and somehow they all knew that I was coming in that night.

*The Latin Kings at this time were well respected in the prison. This organization has its origin in the church, in Chicago. It was a way for the Latin community to help and support one another. However, over time some young knuckle heads distorted what the Kings stood for and what once was something good for the church had spilled out into the streets and became corrupted. It is said a Latin brother named Nelson M., had introduced this mindset into the CTDOC and because of his influence they sent him out of state to do his time.*

### *My thoughts*

" *Think about how you would feel if you had to go dumpster diving every night for your food. This is how I felt having my first experiences with the food being served in the prisons. So, consider this when you are living that life that will potentially bring you to prison for any amount of time. Moreover, think about how my situation could have gotten bad when I had the encounter in the Cheshire C.I. dining hall with this high ranking gang member... I would learn from this experience how to move in the many different chow halls that I would find myself entering throughout the state's prison systems. Over the years I have seen many things happen to people who did not know the laws of the land when it came to prison etiquette.*"

# 4

## TO THYSELF BE TRUE

There are a lot of things that one can do with themselves once they come to prison. Prison comes with its own set of rules and those rules tend to change all depending which game(s) you decide to play during your stay. Let me just name a few of the characters for you that exist so that you can have an idea of the roles individuals play while in prison.

First, you have those that ain't shit, ain't about shit and ain't never going to be shit type of individuals. Those that don't see a need to apply themselves in any manner what-so-ever! The type of individual that would rather run his ass around the block every day for the next 30 days begging for a soup so that he can eat for the next month instead of getting a job in the prison. This is the sorry ass brother that he's asked why he doesn't have a job, he's quick to hit you with some shit like "Shiiiit! I ain't working for these crackers like no slave for no damn dollar a day!" Yet and still this is the same motherfucker that will put his life at risk on those streets and when caught, march his ass back up onto these crackers plantation every fucking chance he gets! These are the worst of the worst in my eyes because they are just taking up the air we breathe and there are others who share the same sentiments.

You have the individual who claims that he has *"Found God!"* since his ass done went and got locked up. I mean in prison there is just one area where multiple religious services take place; but, I am sure that this joker passed by a place of worship on every other block and never once walked inside to give his life to the God of his liking. For the most part these are the individuals who are accused of doing some of the foulest shit on the streets. Now with nowhere to run or hide, he traded in his gun to now tote a bible or Koran everywhere you might see him in the prison. The annoying dude that always greet you with the salutation of "Praise God Brother!" or he's just always trying to get you to breakdown your understanding of the scripture for him because he really can't read; yet, has the uncanny ability to commit to memory what you said and uses your word like a preacher on a hot summer day with a collection plate. I see these individuals often and when they come at me with the bullshit I just shout "Amen my brother, He put you where you praise him the most!!!" See, religion doesn't seem to work for this type of individual on the outside so whenever he feels disconnected from his God he finds his way back to him by committing an act of crime. SMH!

You got the individual who just no longer could take the hand that he was dealt and could no longer take prison; so, to cope with it he runs to the medication line each day and night to self-medicate to avoid the daily reality of being in prison.

You got those con artist/I "keep a Bitch" while doing their bid type of individual. Most times this is either a drug addict or he is your career criminal type individual who has mastered the art of the female chemistry and knows exactly what to say to these women at the right time to make their pussy so wet, they're willing to do anything for this fool. Most time these are the females who are willing to risk their freedom by introducing contraband into the facility to feed his habit.

You got your gambling men. This individual is either the prison bookie or the one who came to prison with a gambling addiction. The bookie has endless prison currency. He's Vegas! The one with the gambling habit, is the one that you will find betting on anything, basketball, football, soccer, or even the finals of the roach race!

Next you got the Al B. Sure type smooth cats that think that they are god's gift to women; *and over a period of time possibly men.* Yeah! Your typical down low type dude. The one you'll see out at the visit with his wife and kids and as soon as he gets back to his block his whole focus has changed. Or you got that type of brother that actor "Terry Crews" played in the movie 'Friday After Next' where he sees Kat William's Character he turns to Ice Cube and says *"fresh fish on the line and I want it…"* Then there's the man who wants other men to call HIM Tammy, Samantha or some other effeminate name that he has come up with for himself. Also, the DOC is now assisting these homosexual men in its facilities in the process of growing breast by supplying them with female growth hormones. This is the type of shit that is tempting a lot of men young and old into committing acts of homosexuality behind these walls. Imagine a grown ass man with some forty double D's in a bra walking around the prison every day? NO! don't do that shit get the vision out of your fucking head…Listen, I'm just saying there's some crazy shit taking place on a daily basis behind these walls like this and I would be remiss and doing my readers a dis-service if I didn't speak about these truths as well.

You have the individual who just wants to do his time and get out of prison. And depending on how he chooses to carry himself, his stay could be easy or it could be hard. In other words, he could very well have been Al B. Sure cell mate! WTF!

You have the pervert; a/k/a/ habitual masturbator, individual who spends his entire bid in lust mode looking for the latest Phat Puff, Straight Stuntin' or Black Video Illustrated magazines. He's like a dog in heat as soon as a female officer or counselor enters the unit. The weird motherfucker who will jerk off or flashes the female officer every time she does her rounds. This is the creep who runs straight to his cell and puts his sign up in his cell window as soon as he sees the nurse inter the unit in those scrubs that look like they were painted on.

You got your art dealers, as I call them. These are the ones' who assist in sustaining the many relationships prisoners have with their woman or children. Ladies, this is where those fancy handkerchief, cards and envelopes come from. Fellas, your girl-friends know you don't have an artistic bone in your body and prior to you getting locked up you hadn't seen a rose in your hood. Regardless to what Tupac said "Roses don't grow from no fuckin' concrete!

You got your official gangsters. These are the individuals who run the gangs from the shadows. You will never see them out in the open drawing unwanted attention to themselves because that is just not their modus operandi when it comes to having a strong hold on their minions. Then you have the type of gang member who is just out there on front street, fronting so that everyone can see them and know who they are. Their family has literally become the individuals they have behind these walls; because they have no contact what-so-ever to the outside world. So, they stay on the gang intelligent officers' radar for doing all types of nonsense throughout the prison and for reasons unbeknownst to me they also enjoy bragging about the countless years they have spent in solitary confinement.

You have the jailhouse lawyer type individual that seems to have the legal acumen to get others out of their situation but could not fight his own way out of a paper bag! These are the individuals that have spent decades studying case law, writing countless writs of habeas corpuses, assisting with parole packages and doing sentence modifications for a fee far below a real attorney's cost. Judges and lawyers are impressed by the tactics used when arguing their case before the courts and most of them give praise at the skill set these men have acquired from within a cage. However, when arguing their own case before the courts they seem to keep getting shut down. It is my personal opinion that this happens because it makes a mockery of the courts when you have an individual that have been deemed functionally illiterate, who come to prison and learn the law in just three or four years' time and shames a seasoned States' Attorney who has held his or her position for the last two or three decades.

You have your hustling type brothers that are just as much about their paper on the inside as they were on the outside. They are into all of the illegal elements in the prison. That was me before I found that you can use that same premise legally and come off financially. I am a natural born hustler; so, hustling behind these walls was like second nature and the money came with ease for me. Once I was on the inside, I wasted no time getting to know the landscape and its major players. Once this knowledge was made known to me, I went to work. See, "*Money is the key to salvation in a capitalist society*" and I'm a capitalist not a socialist; so just know I'm about my money! I would push anything that I could get my hands on that was illegal. I still had some friends that were loyal to me and my struggle on the streets and they were there for me when they saw the fifty-year sentence I had received did not stop me in any way from thinking along the lines of a criminal. I had gotten acquainted with inmates and Correction Officer that were making moves and went to recruiting them to work with me and offered them a greater purse than most because I had it like that. Within no time I was receiving my shipments on a weekly basis.

Whatever there was to be sold in prison that drew a profit I had my hands in it.

### *My thoughts*

 *When you enter into these prison walls there is this magnetic attraction that can pull you in any one of these directions towards becoming one of these types of characters. So, it is very important that you know yourself and stand true to who and what you are because there is always someone in the cut watching and lying in wait to exploit you for whatever weakness that you have exposed them to. Don't get involved with gangs, gambling or homosexuality! These are the three things that will lead you into some bullshit quick fast in the penitentiary. Why? Because joining a gang you will be inheriting some problem that existed years before you came to prison! Gambling, you will one day run the risk of writing the check your ass can't cash!! If you fucking another man in prison it is against the rules and know that countless other men were possibly having sex with this individual before you came into the picture. Plus, NO! MAN! Can replace the feel and touch of a real women; so, whenever you get the urge to release some steam jerkoff!!! – OH! That's against the rules too!"*

# 5

# GIVING ANOTHER GROUP STATUS

When I arrived at Whalley Avenue, there was literally no gangs or gang violence in the county jail that I was aware of during my stay. Grant it, my mind was on all of the shit that I now found myself faced with. Not to mention I was only there a short period of time. I had only spent all of three months at the county jail before I was sentenced and transferred to the newly built Walker Reception Center located in Suffield, Connecticut. Walker C.I., was to be the reception center where all inmates from throughout the State of Connecticut were sent once they were sentenced. When it had open there was a standard that you were only required to stay there for fourteen-days and then be transferred out to do your time at whatever Correctional Institute that you were being sent to base upon your classification level. The inmate classification levels in the Connecticut Department of Correction ranges from level 1 and goes up to a level 5. The higher your classification level was, the more secure the facility you were housed at would be. Level five meant that you were automatically being housed at Northern Correctional Institute, the States' Super-Max prison which houses what the State deems its worst inmates as well as its death row inmates.

Coming into the prison system with a murder charge, I was classified as a level 4 inmate so my first stop along my journey; as a juvenile lifer, would be Cheshire Correctional Institute.

Cheshire Correctional Institute was built in 1910 or 1913, as a reformatory for boys. Historically, it is the second reformatory in the country—with Elmira in the State of New York being the first. I arrived at Cheshire Correctional Institute; a/k/a/ *The ROCK*! in December of 1992. I got in the building at about 3:30am. See, this was before the days of those fifteen passenger vans where you rode the old white modified school bus all night crisscrossing the state until you reached your destination. I was taken through the Admissions process which lasted all of an hour. My clothing and property I had acquired between Whalley Avenue and Walker C.I. was thrown into a trash can on wheels by the Property Officer and then he handed another officer a card with what looked like it had my photo on it. The officer yelled out my name, yo! Was my only response...then he had asked me what was my inmate number, #19-39-19, is all I had to say before this joker told me to step out of the holding cell that held me and all the other new arrivals. We exited the AP Room and took a quick right, then a left onto Two Galley. When I strolled through those gates I entered a world unlike I'd ever seen before. Four tiers stacked upon one another floor to ceiling with Fifty Cells on each tier. The noise reminded me of an animal shelter where you strolled past kennels Stacked yea high on top of each other with men standing there staring at you with their sad faces while the others were barking like dogs, I'm sure there were some pleasurable and terrifying moans from a pussy cat or two as the night past us by!

Hey! Boyd! This officer yelled. I would advise you to stay up under the tier if you don't want nothing thrown on you from up above the officer stated as I pushed the cart. At the end of the second galley were two flights of stairs just outside of the Guard house where I had to bring the portable trash can to an abrupt stop so that I could remove my things. There the corrections officer who escorted me to this point had passed me off to another officer who escorted me up the stairs and all he had to say to me after opening the gate was *"Twelve on Three"*. I still have yet to find out why these officers go out of their way to act tough towards the new arrivals; especially, when a motherfucker just got the rest of his entire life handed to him by the Judge! However, what the officer was striving to say to me was that I was in the twelfth cell on the third galley. I had begun the long but short walk down this narrow hall, about twenty feet and the cell gate (door) slid wide open. I took one step inside, the gate closed behind me and all I can remember thinking was *"WHAT THE FUCK?!"* As I stretched out my arms as they made a cross; with both of my hand touching either side of the walls, I felt like Jesus about to be crucified by the Connecticut Department of Correction.

At Cheshire C.I., the prison runs as if it is a solitary confinement facility. The inmate population is on a status of 22 and 2. What this means is that you are locked in the cell for 22 hours and you are out of the cell for 2 hours. The only exception to this rule was that you had to have a job in the facility if you wanted any extra free time out of the cell. Recreation was given twice a day for an hour. Every morning like clockwork Rec would begin at 8:00am and run to about 9:00am. See, an hour in prison is never actually an hour. It is more like fifty to fifty-five minutes. For some strange reason the time that it took to get off of whatever galley you were on to either the Gym or the Auditorium was always factored into the equation. It's strange because you hardly saw these men who were given the rest of their lives in prison go to the law library. They would much rather play cards or chess then fight for their freedom. However, I later learn that most of the inmate population couldn't read. But, they could damn sure talk a good one!!! LOL!!!

So after the episode in the dining hall at breakfast I returned to my cell with my nerves on edge waiting to get up with those brothers that had saved me from getting into some shit that morning. One Correction Officer work two tiers during this time and was responsible for the hundred or so men living on his tiers. The C.O. standing at the beginning of the tier just an hour into his shift released all of the cells at once by pulling on a lever in this big metal box that hung on the wall which also allowed for him to release the cell doors one at a time if he chose to do so. As my cell door slid open I stepped out unsure of where I was heading; however, I had quickly realized when I came to prison the one thing that I would find myself getting use to was following the crowd in whatever direction they are flowing in. So, that's exactly what I did.

All three hundred pounds of me stepped out of that cell, wearing the mask of a killer as I walked with a confidence that read to anyone who could read my mood… Don't Fuck with Me! I took the stairs into the main hall and looked past all of these new faces as if they didn't mean shit to me nor did they exist in the world that I was now creating for myself. Fifty or so paces, and I had come into contact with a very familiar face from the town.

I approached the familiar face, gave the brother pound as he informed me that everyone else was in the Auditorium. Mark and I were from two different neighborhoods. He was from the Kensington neighborhood; however, we were cool when he was home. He had even spent his last day free out in the world with me before he had to turn his self in to start his bid. We walked in and sat together in the Auditorium while waiting on the rest of the fellas from the home town to arrive. The Auditorium was an old movie theater; but, the projector didn't work so up on the stage was a big 55-inch television that no one paid attention to except those who didn't have a t.v. in their cell. While Mark and I were chilling on the bench, he began to give me the drop on everything that had been going on with the fellas before my arrival and also a little on how the facility ran.

Mark was the brother who just wanted to do his time and get out without encountering any problems along the way. By no means was he what we would call a shooter where I am from; because he didn't like gun play at all. On the streets you would want to hang with Mark to just fuck a bitch! He played the club scene heavy and was known for getting money; so, the females loved him. Therefore, you would most certainly be guaranteed to fuck one of the friends of a chick he was knocking off if you were in his company.

He was the first one to tell me that fucking with a jailhouse gang would be a bad move for me. He schooled me to the fact that all the guys from New Haven were now a part of a gang called the Elm City Boys (ECB) which was hard for me to comprehend at first because we're talking about niggas that are some natural born killers who were just head hunting each other when they were out on the streets. I just could not fathom some shit like this ever happening...EVER!

In New Haven, during this time there existed a lot of different crews from all over the city and these individuals either represented their neighborhoods or their drug territories. There were five primary hoods that would come from the surrounding New Haven area. That is The Hill (the hood that I come from), Newhallville, West Hills, Fair Haven, and The Kensington neighborhoods.

So many lives were lost on the streets of New Haven due to these drug wars during the mid to late 80's and most of those that were charged and convicted of these crimes were now serving their time throughout the state's prison system. Somehow, the masterminds of this organization thought it would be a brilliant idea for all of these drug dealers, robbers, and murderers; who were suspected of the killing of each other's families and friends, to relinquish all existing beef that they had on the streets -*regard-*

*less to what side of town you came from or what crew you use to represent on the outside-* and band together within the prison walls to become this unforeseen force to be reckoned with.

During the mid to late 1980s, the money from the drug trade in New Haven was flowing like crazy and we had a body count like no other city in the State. Visitors from out of town thought that they were running the risk of being shot if they came to New Haven to club or hangout. New Haven was even affectionately known as "Money craving, Pistol waving New Haven!" there was this lust for violence and money in the town. So, the fact that so many murderers were coming together from New Haven within the prison literally struck fear in the hearts of the other gangs as they began to see us rolling deep. And when I say deep, I am not talking about in numbers either. See, that never really mattered to us. What mattered the most was that we had the motherfucking heart that it took to go up against any other known force in the prison! We didn't give a fuck what the opposition's number count was; because, we were gonna show up to any challenge and show the fuck out. Just so you know, showing the fuck out meant that by the time we were done the prison was sure to be placed on lockdown for some time afterwards.

Vividly, I can remember having a conversation with Mark as he was striving to pull my coat to what was going on in that prison and the formation of the gang culture that was developing. *"Yo! Ray listen, these dudes know how you get down and are going to try to get you to run with the click that they are forming in here. Don't get involved in any of that shit man I'm telling you... just focus on doing your time and over turning your case so you can get the fuck up outta here."-* is what Mark said to me. Oh! I heard this nigga loud and clear, but I wasn't listening to a fucking word that he had to say to me. I had just been given a life fucking sentence, what the fuck is a nigga like me to be looking forward in a physical hell?

I literally paid him no mind because I knew Mark and in

knowing him, I always knew that if it came to getting violent he didn't want any problems. This was his motto on the streets and was how he was playing in the prison system as well. Violence in prison differs from violence on the streets on so many different levels. Violence behind these prison walls is more of an up close and personal type of situation. In prison you were made to face down your enemy and go into hand to hand combat if need be. You had nowhere to run or hide. Also, stabbing another man is some up close and personal shit. It's nothing like shooting a man on the streets from a distance... and shooting from a distance is what most men who had bodies were in prison for.

So, I avoided his advice and after a while I became involved with ECB as well as all the other bullshit that came along with it. My introduction to the gang culture did not come by way of what most would normally see on Television or hear about in other States. I was not jumped in nor was I asked to do some crazy shit to prove myself to anyone. The founders were very aware of how I was moving out on the streets prior to my incarceration and they saw the love that I was receiving when I got there. So pretty much, my reputation had superseded me in that sense. I didn't even have to start as a foot soldier within the ranks and this left somewhat of a bitter taste in the mouths of a few brothers who felt as though they were there from the beginning so they should be holding a position within the "family." Behind closed door in discussions with the leaders, their thoughts to me was always *"Fuck them niggas' Ray, we run this shit! And if they have a problem with who we give the positions to let them bring it to us."* Doing some shit like this would surely get you ostracized; so, a lot of times this expressed dissatisfaction was spoken to someone you thought you were cool with – and I say "thought" because the shit always made it back to the top and they would find themselves being checked about some shit they said but was never willing to say they said.

The inner workings of the gang life are strange like that. You have all types of individuals running with you. Crack heads and dope fiends who were just months off the streets and rehabbed to some degree and were dying for the opportunity to be put in the position to where they would have the power to give orders to the brother whose drugs they were willing to trade their little sister for just a short time ago. These types of men were never given a position in the ranks because they were weak natured individuals. Having a dope or crack habit automatically disqualified you from the aforementioned. If the administration got wind that a dope head was holding any high position they would exploit this opportunity at turning him into a jailhouse snitch. They would literally give him a bag of dope or coke that they had confiscated from another inmate in a shakedown of his person or cell and try to turn him.

### *My thoughts*

*Since mid-1996, I left that gang shit alone and became an advocate against gangs and gang violence in the prison and on the streets. When I say that I walked away from it that is exactly what I did and did not care what a motherfucker thought about it. I was out and wasn't nothing or no one stopping me. I had become the man that I was destined to be and stood on my own two feet. Oftentimes I find myself engaged in conversation with active gang members and for some reason they are always trying to justify being on the bullshit. So, I will just pick out the foulest individual who they are calling their brother and ask "will you bring this nigga to your house around your moms and kids for dinner?" 99.99% of the time the answer is NO! I then ask well why in the hell are you calling this dude your brother and putting your life on the line for him? See, I been through the bullshit in that life and I advocate that fucking with a gang is the biggest illusion of love that one can be sold on in the prison industry complex. These niggas ain't ya family! This shit has cost a lot of people their lives. Your family are those who have been supporting you while you are serving your sentence so if you are considering joining a gang you need to not only think about the hurt that you can potentially be bringing to yourself, but think about your family."*

# 6

## A HUSTLER'S SPIRIT...

I n the streets when a man goes to prison there is a saying that is used to describe the loss of his freedom and it is stated that *"the game doesn't change, only the players!"* What this actually means is that the players in the game will eventually meet either one of the two demises that are directly associated with playing the game and none of them ever involve anyone winning. But, you will either end up *'Dead or in Jail!'* Well, upon my arrival to prison I found that the drug game was alive and flourishing in prison as far as I was concerned. So, I guess the phrase rings true to a degree because behind these walls nothing had truly changed.

However, I know one thing for sure is that I instantly became one of the new players on the scene. This position was a very inorganic one as I now look back on it; because, all I actually wanted to do was smoke some weed and let my time pass away with my head in the clouds. When I first came to prison I had a lot of shit on my mind. Besides this fresh fifty-year's sentence I had; which there was no idea as to how I was going to start it nor end it! I had a newborn son at home that I wasn't going to have a hand in rearing. Yeah! I said rearing. We raise animals, while as parents we rear our children. Plus, there was the family and friends whom I didn't know when I would see them again. So many of them have passed on over the years that I have desensitized myself to death so that I no longer have to deal with the pain that is associated with losing someone that I had love for.

So, as time would pass by and word had gotten around the prison from some of the old heads that I smoked with from time to time that I was holding some of the best smoke the prison had seen in some time. This I could clearly understand due to the fact that I was fresh into the system; however, with one foot fresh in the penitentiary and the other foot still on the street because I possessed this insatiable desire to continue hustling even while in prison! What The Fuck was I thinking? I know! However, I still had several reliable friends out there on the streets whom I could depend on and they were moving hundreds if not thousands of pounds of weed weekly. These were some of the men that I ran with when I was out and they were especially empathetic to my current status of being inmate #193919 and having a fifty-year sentence handed to me. So much so, these men would pretty much give me anything that I would ask for during this time with no questions asked. In their minds they may have felt as though this was the least that they could do. They even may have felt like they were easing some of the suffering that I was experiencing; as I served out my time, by prescribing me a quarter or half pound of weed at my every request.

I had heard how most of the drugs being sold were being introduced into the prison during this time and I personally didn't want any parts of smoking something that was smuggled in someone else's ass. Prisoners would grease their asses in order to insert balloons filled with contraband into the facility. Who the fuck came up with this idea, I don't want to know! I would hear that some dudes wanted to get high so bad that they would smoke this shit "literally" and then be like 'Yo! I'm not dealing with him no more because when I rolled my joint it smelt and tasted like shit!' Yet this asshole still smoked it…I just knew that it would not be me. So, I knew that I had to find out how I could make some solid hand-to-hand transactions and not the ass-to-mouth ones that others were doing. I never made moves through the visiting room for these reasons. Plus, I knew that there was only but so much drugs a nigga could put up his ass, that is, until I saw a show on television that showed the x-rays of a drug mule and how much drugs this idiot was holding in his intestines. This just never appealed to me.

There were several Corrections Officers from my city who were familiar with who I was, or who I ran with on the streets from reading the newspapers or through word of mouth, or either just from seeing me in the city when I was free. There are a lot of Correction Officers from the hood; be it New Haven, Hartford, Bridgeport or any other small urban city, who keep it real and are fond of the kids from their cities that were making things happen out on those streets getting money. Most times these Officers grew up around your way or on the same block that most of us grew up on and they will fuck with you on the strength of that alone. Of course you got those who fuck with you just so that they can go home at night and pillow talk to their wives or girlfriends about how they either fuck with the nigga that was getting money on so & so block or how fucked up he treats the motherfucker now that a nigga is in a fucked up position. Once a real nigga is removed from the streets, this affords that lame Correctional Officer who always wanted to live the life and couldn't get a Girl or even fuck a side chick.

I have six brothers and three sisters all of whom are older than me; so, I had come to learn that most of these Correction Officers' went to school at some point with my family member or frequented a nightclub with them. This gave me an advantage over the rest of those who were making moves in the prison. I had access to a number of the staff who would eventually start working for me. I never used the same officer twice and made sure that I kept them in an even rotation so that they didn't have to go looking for work from anyone else in the prison. I would even make moves when I didn't have to to ensure that they had that extra cash in their pockets to play with. Four-hundred extra dollars in their pockets a week for fifteen minutes of work meant they didn't have to work any overtime to pay off their bills but could stay at home and enjoy themselves.

Holding onto so much smoke led to me selling five or ten dollar pieces for commissary. However, over time there is only so much food you can eat or cosmetics you can use which led me to eventually selling larger pieces for cash only! In prison drugs that are sold for cash only usually came in the form of a money order being sent to someone on the outside, the cash being dropped off at a residence on the outside or some guy would smuggle cash in on a visit to buy what they wanted. I had even had family members of the buyer give the money to my visitor when they left the visit and I would serve them when we got back to the housing unit. The money that I started to see meant a lot to me because it was able to ease the financial burden I had put on my sons' mother and the rest of my family. In a matter of no time, I was the one that everybody wanted to deal with because they knew that I would treat them right by giving them what their dollar could buy. While the other inmates that were moving shit in their asses were limited in the quantity of drugs they had. I had the weight on smash…and as they say now-a-days, I was the plug!

Seeing this, I was determined to win by all means. I also knew that getting into the drug business in prison would be some next level shit for me and if I played the game right it could potentially become very lucrative for me in the long run. A bag of dope that went for ten dollars on the street, was going for fifty dollars in the prison. One of the first things that I had to commit myself to doing in choosing this way of life was not taking no shorts from anyone what-so-ever! Not when it came to the money and I could not let anyone slide on anything disrespectful. *Or at least that's what I had thought early on...we'll get to that later. Because, I'd come to find that I had to change if I wanted to continue to win.*

Weed was my thing at first. However, that shit is too bulky and there isn't that many places to stash weed in prison. So, a lot of times I was left holding that shit on my person all of the time or I would bag it up and pay other inmates to hold it in their cells for me. Whenever I did this I had to find the individual who was never on the radar of the Correction Officers, or the individual whom I knew was so in with the Correction Officers that the officer wouldn't shake their cells down. There was also the motherfucker who just didn't give a fuck about anything so he was down for whatever, even if it meant holding a half pound of bagged up fifty pieces of weed in his cell for me, getting caught with it, and catching a new charge. You'd be surprised at how many dudes are willing to go through this just so they can brag about getting knocked off. This shit creates his-story! And prison is big in the art of storytelling. I preferred to lay in the shadows; but, prison provides no place for no man to hide. So as low key as I tried to be the more I was put under the radar of the prison intelligence team.

Yeah! The Intelligence team stayed running up in my cell and the cells of those that I dealt with looking for gang shit (because of my past) or drugs. I didn't fuck with gangs or any of that so-called family shit because that shit was a fallacy and nothing came from it but a fucking headache. I damn sure wasn't getting caught with no drugs because I wasn't trying to add on to the time that I was already doing. So, I had to find some sure shot spots to hide my shit because I was not in the habit of taking losses. I was living on the south side of the prison in unit one, in the first cell. The officers' station was just outside my door and it was elevated so that the officer could see directly into my spot anytime he or she felt like it.

My cellmate during this time was a kid named Prince from around my way on Congress Avenue who used to get money with my brother King Bee, back in the early 80's. Prince also was a worker of mine in the early 90's before I came in. I really liked this brother because he was a natural born hustler who was more than willing to hug the block all day and all night no matter the weather to bring in that money. When he worked for me, it didn't take me long to find out several things about him that handicapped his hustle game that I wasted no time in exploiting. He never took the time to learn the ins and outs of the game. I used to front two kids from around my way 4½ to 9 oz. of coke a day depending on how I felt on any given day. I thought Prince was ready to step his game up because he had proved to be loyal when it came to moving the bundles on the block. However, I had given him several ounces of coke one time and when he went to the table with the work to do his thing I'd learn that bagging up was foreign to him and he had never even touched a triple beam scale in his life. Everything he had ever sold out on the street was already pre-packaged for him. One day I had asked him to make a run for me in my car and learned that he couldn't even drive. So, you guessed it this kid would only be good for posting up on the block. Other than that I literally had no use for him.

Prince and I, had both secured jobs in the south block hallway because I had a plan in the works as to where I may be able to stash the bulk of weed that I was holding. My plan was to put this weed right up under their noses. There are two bathrooms off of the south block hallway and one had a cabinet in it that held the chemicals used to keep these rooms clean and I had figured that there was no way that the officers would shake their own bathrooms down if some shit was to ever pop off in the facility. So, I had to make sure that the cabinet stayed stocked with endless chemicals, paper towels, hand soap and toilet paper. They had this chemical "Babble" that was like a cheap version of Ajax that we used at home to scrub the toilets with to get the bowl clean. The Babble was a powdered substance but came in a half gallon milk like carton that I would empty and replace with my drugs two thirds of the way.

We were allowed to go out there whenever we wanted to in order to clean the staff bathrooms or sweep and mop the floors. So whenever I needed to make a sell; I would take the orders, we would go out into the hall as if we were going to clean something and dip into the bathroom and go into the stash and get whatever it was that was needed at the time. Because there were so many cleaning supplies in this room it would disguise and cover up the strong smell of the weed.

Now, there were some other brothers from the town who were getting their weed from dudes that I hung with while on the streets and these were the same guys that would supply me with what I wanted whenever I wanted it. Because these guys were paying for what I was getting for free, I had the upper hand on them. This meant that I could offer up more weed then they could; so, my quarters and fifties were always bigger than theirs. In no time I had captured their clientele and had customers coming from all over the facility to get their hands on some of that good shit. Of course it caused a rift between myself and these brothers but I'm a capitalist not a socialist. So, my concern was on my money; therefore, I could give a rats' ass about the next niggas feelings or how he felt about how I was moving!

I had worked my program for several years up until the Department of Correction found ways to interrupt the flow of money out of the facility via their inmate account system. The system ran like this, an inmate would get a special request form from the counselor and fill the form out stating the amount of money to be removed from their inmate account, the name of the person that they would like the funds sent to and give this slip to the counselor along with an envelope. The counselor would then send this information off to the inmate accounts office where a check would be cut and shipped out.

For some time, this put a dent in the game and everybody that was hustling in the prison was feeling the loss. Nobody knew what their next move would be; but, I knew that I had to come up with something quick to circumvent their system...and I did just that! See, I was investing the cash that I was making from the sales on these drugs into stocks with several companies. I had got put on to making these investments from some of the older prisoners that were customers of mines. They would always say to me that I should invest my money in a DRIP program with all of the time I was serving. The DRIP program was a **Dividends Re-Investment Program** where the dividends that you made each quarter would be reinvested into more shares. These dudes had life and it seemed like their money was just as endless as their time was. And to the best of my knowledge I was the only one taking my proceeds and doing this. I had found a way where I could white out my name from the investment invoice and only utilize the Number on the invoice to make deposits into my accounts. Once I had ran a test run using my own money I knew this would work for anyone else. I went to the library the next week, grabbed the typewriter, and typed in *"Please Deposit These Funds into My Account! Thank You!"*, then went up to the copier manned by a prisoner to have him run off about fifty copies of the document and went back into doing business. I would not dare share this finding with the rest who were getting money and most of them were afraid of taking chances with investing their money into the stock market. Hell! We were already in prison so we didn't have to give two fucks about risk versus reward. This was most definitely a way for me to make some passive income for myself.

I did this for just about two years before I had come up with my next idea. I had to find new ways of getting the money off these jokers' books and into my pockets. So, I had come up with an idea of starting my own shell company as a way of getting the money. However, this would require the assistance from someone on the outside whom I could really trust with a large sum of money. I would ask a friend of mine if she'd be willing to assist me and she was down after I had spoken my first words. All she said was *"Tell me what I gotta do and you know I got you!"* I explained to her how the process would work.

"First, I would have to start my own LLC. Therefore, I would need her to find a registered agent for me before she would be able to move forward with the filing of the proper paperwork with the Connecticut Secretary of States' office in order to be recognized as a legitimate limited liability company. This is when Lost Tri-State Investments was born. I had figured that no one from the intelligence team would ever question someone making an investment especially if they researched the company and had come to find it to be a legitimate entity. Then in the next step she would have to file for a federal tax identification number with the Internal Revenue Services. Once the filing was done and she received the number, I had instructed her to open up a business account with the bank in the company name. She then needed to go to the local post office at the corners of Hallock street and Washington Avenue and open up a post office box to receive the mail that was about to start flowing in. I had explained to her that each year it would be her responsibility to file an income tax for the money that I was bringing in and I further told her that she would be able to keep whatever the return was for the year. This was music to her ear and she got a kick out of the fact that I; a 'nigga' from the streets with little to no education, was thinking on the level I was thinking on when it came to getting this money. She would later express to me "Ra'-sun, these niggas out here need to take a page out of your play book God; because you are definitely what the streets have been missing!" I just smile on the other end of the phone, because I already knew my own self-worth and I knew what the streets were in for when I got there. No! They weren't going to get another drug dealer. However, they were going to see a mogul being released from these prison walls!!!

The game was changing in prison for me as I had moved away from selling weed and started pushing dope. At first the dope game wasn't something that I wanted to do because I had grown up on the Congo (Congress Avenue), where if this block were a jungle I saw firsthand how dope could ravage the human body as feigns walked the block with the arms the size of Gorillas. Not to mention the abscesses that erupted and exposed the raw flesh up under their skin. However, one of my friends who was visiting me kept me informed with how things were changing on the streets. He informed me that the dope game out on the streets was killing them and had everybody wanting to get in on it. He was telling me that kilos of dope were cheap and the profit margins on the comeback were higher than any amount of weed he was getting. So, any and everybody had dope on the streets. So much so, the block now reminded him of a scene out of American Gangster when Frank Lucas had 116th Street and Lenox Avenue on lockdown with blue magic. It was during this talk with him that I had decided to get my hands in the mix. However, I knew that I had to be careful because one could easily become a dope head if you allowed the fumes to inter your system while bagging up.

I returned from my visit and went to recreation and sat with some of my trusted ole' heads from around my block. I told them what I was thinking and what my next move would be and how I was going to need them to be on board with what I was about to introduce to the facility. South block one was putting a big restriction on my movement; so, I had told the fellas that I was going to reclassify my job assignment to the kitchen because I needed to have access to the entire facility at all times. Little did I know, this move would prove to be the best thing for me and the hustle I was putting down on this camp? The kitchen presented me the opportunity to reach everybody in the prison undetected. At this time the facility was feeding in the main dining hall and all six units in the south and east blocks came to the chow hall while the kitchen was responsible for taking the food to the north blocks in food carts. The food carts meant that I could literally walk into the north blocks on third shift while the block officer was half asleep and make moves. The guys from the south and east sides I served as they came through the chow line to grab their food. I did this while an officer stood right outside of the feeding windows. While the officers' focus was on making sure no one got away with getting an extra tray, I would move forty or fifty bags of dope a day up under their noses.

My transition into the dope game was well received by the Correctional Officers that I now had on payroll because they didn't have to move a pound of weed through the Officers check point. Seven grams of compressed raw heroin could fit into the palm of their hands. Little did they know they were holding onto a goldmine! My first shipment had arrived and I went to work to making sure I killed them…figuratively of course. On the streets a gram of dope goes for about one hundred dollars but each gram of dog food (as dope was affectionately referred to in prison) that I got cost me nothing; so, again I was one up on the next cat that was trying to do his thing in the prison. On the streets a bag goes for $10. In prison a bag goes for anywhere from $25 to $50. Depending on who you dealt with and how it was introduced into the facility. If it came in through the visit, you were sure to pay towards the high end. I was letting my shit go for $35 a bag. Off of every gram of dog food bagged up you can get about thirty-five bags. I only wanted to see thirty bags off of every gram. So, not only were my bags bigger but I was letting them go for less than the average price. A bundle which is ten bags I'd let go for three-hundred-dollars. Customers were dying to get to me and cop the shit I had before I ran out. My first flip had me riding on a cloud. I had cleared 6,300.00 and after seeing this there was no stopping me. I spent over sixteen years in the kitchen on and off; so, you do the math! This shit was reminding me of a verse from one of Jay-Z's songs where he spits *"I'm a hustler, fuck that! Correctional Facilities can't correct that!"* I lived by the mantra for so long and brought in so much cash it was crazy living this kind of life behind these walls.

Over time I knew that I had to move on to something else because all good things must come to an end. So, before I was busted by the intelligence team I threw in my hat. However, I had come to find that there are only but so many addicts in prison and I knew that whatever I chose to do it had to be something that was all inclusive. I had to get into some shit that would warrant the whole prison dealing with me...

What man doesn't want to smell good? Oils! When I first came to prison Muslim oils were nothing to come by, we could buy those good oils from commissary when I was up north at the prison (Somers). However, as the Department of Correction began to get a hold on the inmate population they started to implement rules and regulations to gain order in their facilities. They centralized all of the commissary for the state. Then over time they stopped ordering Muslim oils from the Muslim shop in Hamden, Connecticut and started getting some watered down shit from the commissary vendor Keefe. No one wanted to wear this oil to a visit so it was only being used to keep the cells smelling good or covering up weed smoke.

Now there were others who were doing their thing in this department; but, again they weren't doing it on the level that I would come to do it. I saw that the guy who had the oil only had one or two types of ...three at best. This meant that his customers were not being exposed to variety and because of this they would only be incline to spend but so much money on the oils. Seeing this, I made it my business to have my people order me several catalogs for vendors that sold Muslim oils. I was looking to deal with the company that had the best oils at the best price. I copped from Garden of fragrances, Gold Star Imports and Madina on Atlantic Avenue in Brooklyn, New York. Garden of Fragrance became my supplier of the oil that I was pushing. They had some quality oils at a price that would turn me a good profit.

Several times I had the opportunity of going into the oil business with a few guys in the prison; but, I looked at oils as a small time hustle that wasn't for me at the time even though each ounce of oil was going for $25.00. When the offers were made to me I was given the ins and outs on how it was run. Every pound of oil yielded 16 one ounce bottles. Ah! Ha! I started to tell myself that I did not have to buy pound bottles because they were too bulky for one and if I purchased one-hundred-ounce bottle of oil at $3.99 a pop and sold them for $25.00, I would move more because I could provide a variety and off of that hundred ounce I would clear $2,500.00. The facility holds over 1,300 inmates so I knew that I could sell out with no problem. If I could average 100 bottles a week in a years' time I could bring in $30,000.00. Now that's above livable wages on the outside. Who would have known that coming to prison could be so lucrative? Not me! SMILE!

I experienced years of this type of shit with them Intel boys breathing down my back. I never suffered a loss, never was I charged for none of my illicit activities behind these prison walls. So, I knew that if I didn't cut the shit my days were numbered. I begin to look at life through a different lens. One that showed me that I could use my God given talents to do good if I'd only stop finding ways to get over on the system. I felt like the opposite to Sylvester Stallone's character in the movie Escape Plan where he was finding the flaws in the prisons security system and breaking out, I was finding flaws in their system and bringing contraband in.

### *My thoughts*

*Over the course of my incarceration, I have come to realize that you cannot find a geographical cure for a disease that exist within your mind...Meaning until you looked within and did some introspection that allowed you to dig deep within and rid your mind of all of the unlikeable thing that have brought you to prison in the first place you will continue to live a life of suffering and recidivism. Far too often I hear motherfuckers say that when they get out they are moving to Atlanta, GA, Charlotte, NC., or some other southern state as if there ain't shit poppin' in those country ass towns. Shit! Last I checked there has always been niggas and bitches trying to get a fresh start at life in the south. But when they get there they see that nothing has changed but the Geographic's because in these small enclaves you are sure to find a bunch of city motherfuckers who thought that they were escaping the bullshit that they were going through in the north by moving down south. But many have digressed back into their old ways. Prison can only become a place of reform and transformation if a motherfucker can get it into his or her head that they are completely done with the bullshit that they were associated with on those streets! Yeah! I got it, but it damn sure took several years for the shit to sink into my head that I was playing Russian roulette behind enemy lines; because, someone could have very easily overdosed on the drugs that I was pushing in the prison or I could have been busted for selling those drugs and potentially had consecutive time added on to the time that I was already serving. So, learn from my experiences and don't make some of the decisions that I made in my*

*past because you can be setting yourself up to receive a life sentence if someone overdosed off of some shit that is out there on those streets today. Jay-Z said "I'm a hustler, fuck that! Correctional facilities can't correct that!" what he was striving to convey to you is if you have a hustlers' spirit that is something that is innate. All you have to do is project that hustle towards doing something legitimate with your hustle game. At this juncture I chose to write these books and hustle like this and take whatever cash I make from the sales and invest it into something else that will bring in some income for me."*

# 7

# GETTIN' IT COOKIN' IN THA' KITCHEN

G rowing up, I always made it my business to spend time at my mom's house during the holidays. It seemed like everybody in my neighborhood that knew me or either one of my brothers or sisters would stop by for a plate of moms' cooking. Since I wasn't the only one of her boys getting money, we made sure that every table was covered with one of mom's special dishes. Ever since I was a kid, I would sit around my mom's playing the kitchen whenever she would be chef-in-it-up licking the cake bowls and all of the other kid shit that I could get away with while keeping her company.

My mother would always stay up late nights cooking for the holidays; so, I would break night with her and I always took mental notes on how to make the things that she was making. See, I knew that this would score me some points with the ladies one day. Yeah! It did. Just ask my ex-wife about the time I stopped her when she went to pick up that can of readymade gravy in the supermarket. Mom dukes is from Charleston, South Carolina and she ain't never fed none of her kids no damn gravy out of no can!

So when we got back to the house, I went into the kitchen,

clean the chicken we had purchased, seasoned it with flour, salt and some black pepper, shook it up in that brown paper bag the exact way momma showed me how to and fried it up in that cast iron pan for ten minute on each side. When I was finished, I removed about 80% of the grease from the pan and cut up one large onion, threw it in the pan to sauté for about a good seven minute on a medium heat until those onions were caramelized, then I put in several table spoons of flour with a cup and a half of water and let that thing cook for another fifteen minutes before pouring it over that chicken and rice. We ate and then I got ready for some pussy...Hey! I'm just saying that's the reward I got! Smile! If the way to someone's heart is through his stomach, I can assure you that the same way that I benefited from cooking her my mom's gravy, she is now benefiting from my teaching her how to make my moms' gravy! There's a brother right now who is thankful for the work I put in.

I mention this simply to say that I always had skills when it came to cooking in the kitchen. So as my hustle evolved over time, I switched jobs and got reclassified to the kitchen block. The block that housed all of the kitchen workers was located in South Block Three. Low and behold this would become the spot to be in so many ways. If the movie New Jack City had the Carter Building, then my equivalent was the kitchen. I sold just about everything out of the kitchen. I was the fucking Jeff Bezos of Cheshire Correctional Institute and my Amazon warehouse was located in the chow hall.

In no time flat I had won over the kitchen supervisors. They loved me to say the least. Why? Because I was very different from the rest of the fellas that they had to encounter and deal with on a daily basis. One I have always had and shown respect for those in authority. Very early on I had learned to speak the language of the people; so, my vernacular was not full of street slang and profanity. Nor was my conversation centered on gossip; therefore, they knew that when they engaged me in conversation they would walk away from me learning something that they did not know or something that they never took the time to recognize. Also, we shared the same passion---FOOD! Given this fact I was able to win them over because I would always allow them to teach me something that they thought I did not know...why would a student ever reveal to his teacher that the teacher ain't teaching him shit? The teacher will lose all interest in the student and I needed them to take a certain level of interest in me if I were to prosper with my new plan.

I had become an avid reader so I was reading everything I got my hands on when it came to cooking. So, I would mention certain dishes to the supervisors and they would be surprised that I knew that dish but could properly pronounce it as well. To them I was some fucking alien from outer space because this just wasn't what they were used to seeing on a normal basis in the prison. One day there was talk amongst myself and one of the supervisors about the best way to prepare a fillet Mignon. Well, the very next day I was called into the office and handed a bag containing four Fillet Mignon, a bottle of A-1 steak sauce, a small tub of sour cream, one red onion and told to cook them up. I walked out of that office and went to work at making a first impression on the supervisors. By the time I walked back into their office, I had baked the fillet mignon medium rare with sauté red onions on top, along with baked potatoes topped with butter & sour cream and a salad on the side.

Having read that presentation is everything because people eat with their eyes, I did all within my power to make them think that they had gotten their meal at a five-star takeout restaurant.

Phase one of my plan was complete. I had got them to give me my personal seat at their table. Any time you can get a staff member to see you as a human, you have an advantage point to operate from. This is why the administration trains its staff not to fraternize with the inmate population...they don't want you to benefit from the relationship. This jewel was reaffirmed for me when I read the book "New Jack: Guarding Sing Sing." In the book the *Tome*, the author went undercover and exposed why the New York Department of Corrections trains its Correction Officers not to get close to the prisoner that they are responsible for overseeing. However, this dyadic relationship is kind of hard to avoid in this state because all the prisons are within 20 miles of a major city. My city was just fifteen minutes down the road from the prison, and yes DOC hired a lot of men & women as Correctional Officers from the City of New Haven and HELL YES I benefited from these relationships!

I really needed these cats working here to see me as their equal. One time one of these cats didn't show up for work and I had found out that his wife had went into labor and was having their child at Yale New Haven Hospital. I made a call home (via the mobile air ways) and had my sister; who worked at the hospital take over about five hundred in baby clothing. Did he turn it down? Emphatically No! He actually thought it was the realist thing that an inmate can do. Especially since I was doing fifty-years. But I knew what he didn't and that was one day it would all payoff to my benefit.

In any prison that I have done time in they all know that I am one hell of a Cook and Baker. Hell, they even know that I got skills up at the Department of Correction headquarters. I know that you are probably wondering to yourself where am I going with this, right? Well, the kitchen would become my central distribution spot. This may be hard for a lot of people to believe; but, I was loansharking in this bitch. I paid for so many beauty salon trips or trips to Kim Chin's so that they can get their mani-pedi done its ridiculous. I covered the cost of so many fantasy football games it makes no sense.

I slung so much Weed, Dope, Coke, Dust and Oils right up under their noses. The crazy thing about it all was the more that I became known for my Cooking and baking skills the more the officers came out of the wood works to get a taste. Most of them knew that I was with the bullshit in the facility! But because I wasn't stabbing or killing nobody, they chose to look past my dealing for a hot plate of food at lunch. They were even informing me of when the intelligence team had me on their radar. The cell that I was in kept getting shook down by the Intel-boyz and they were steadily coming up empty handed. This shit was frustrating the hell out of them to the point the Warden himself was fed up with my shit and had me transferred out of "his" facility. Shit, I was making half of his salary just doing my time! If I was in his shoes, I'd do the same thing to me. When this had happened, several officers tried to come to my aide and it was stated to me that he flipped out on them saying "Boyd, can walk out of that kitchen and down the halls with a knife and none of you will attempt to stop him. So, he's out of here!" his request would be short lived and I would be back in "his" prison back at it in just four months' time.

My next reign would last all of fourteen months before I was caught up in a conspiracy and allegedly accused of robbing the commissary of three thousand dollars a week for a period of just over twenty-five weeks. So, you do the math. For the record I was never found guilty of anything associated with the afore-mentioned; but. I will tell my readers that I ate well! LMAO! Wink! I was transferred this time with a DO NOT RETURN HIS BLACK ASS TO CHESHIRE C.I. in my file.

### *My thoughts*

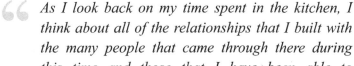

*As I look back on my time spent in the kitchen, I think about all of the relationships that I built with the many people that came through there during this time and those that I have been able to maintain over the years. I often ask myself was it all worth it and a lot of times my answer to myself is*

*conflicting because I should have chosen another path upon my arrival to prison. However, I had to take this path or else I would not be penning the prose so that someone else can avoid the road that I chose to travel and take the one less traveled when they find themselves in my situation. Oh! The money's all gone so don't look for it to last that long. Make better choices with your life and how you do your time. Put your energy in fighting for your freedom and getting home and I can guarantee you that you'll appreciate the work that you put in on yourself especially when you can see that it wasn't wasted."*

# 8

## FRESH AS HELL

Over the years in prison, the administration had moved away from allowing the inmate population from having things sent into the prison. There was once a time when anyone with the means to do so could pretty much order whatever they wanted and have it shipped in. No matter what prison you found yourself in, everyone in Connecticut knew that dudes from New Haven were known to keep all of the fly feet (sneakers) when they came out. That's just what we were known for and sometimes this shit brought on the hate from niggas that were jealous of how we got down when it came to our image. Brothers from Bridgeport did their thing. Brothers from Hartford were a little slow with how they were moving. They were all purchasing their sneakers from the same sneaker store and this is where they would go to get their Shell Toe Adidas or a fresh pair of suede Puma's. The store was called Herbs. I know this brother got rich off of the cats from Hartford. New Haven had mad sneaker store that we could purchase our foot ware from. We had J&M's on Grand Avenue, Running Start on Whitney Avenue and Trumbull Street, Athlete Foot & Foot Locker in the mall, and of course the Famous Sport Stuff on Whalley Avenue. Sport Stuff had become famous during the early 1990's when within the first three months in business they had released an article in the New Haven register that they had made over $250,000.00 and they were literally putting their competition out of business. To the point where other sneaker stores like *Body and Sole* located on Chapel Street were posting in the windows of their establishments that "Drug Money was not welcome". But by the time these posting were posted, the damage was already done and those motherfuckers were having a going out of business sale.

If you walked into someone's cell from New Haven, you would be met by a variety of feet lining the cell wall from the front door of the cell to the rear near the window. Our style was very distinct from that of everyone else, you could tell which town someone was from; literally, by the sneakers that they wore. If you saw dudes walking the halls on their way to the chow hall, gym, yard, or visit and all they had on were shell toe Adidas with different color strips or pumas, you automatically knew they were from Hartford. If you saw a group; with their swagger on one thousand, walking through the halls like they owned the prison and you took a look at their feet game instantly you knew that we were not playing any fucking games. You would see all kinds of Jordan's, Bo Jacksons, Iverson's, Stan Smiths, Sam Cassel's, Rodman's and all that other fly shit.

Every year New Haven dudes had to have the latest Jordan's or any other athletic name brand sneaker when they first came out. But, them J's was at the top of everybody's list. Also, if you were from the town you knew the importance of having a fresh pair of wheat colored Timberland Boots to rock on the visit. Nothing looked better than a Crisp Tan prison uniform and some fresh Tim's to match. The ladies loved seeing us come through that visiting room door as if we never missed a beat out there on those streets. The visiting room in prison is known as the *Dance Floor*. It was given this name because most brothers in prison got ready for their visits as if they were about to hit the club up and dance all night. No one goes to the club looking like a dummy!!!

When I was getting all of this money in prison I found ways to spend it on some things that I like or that I thought would assist in making my bid go by a lot faster. So, I had to have all of the luxuries that my money could buy and I went hard when it came to spending cash on me. I can remember when Jay-Z came out with the S. Carters Reebok that reminded me of the Gucci sneakers from back in the days. I was sitting in the cell telling my little man about the Gucci sneakers because he had never seen them. Then a month would past and I came across an ad in the XXL magazine. Those shits were so fly I had to have them. So I put in the order with my peoples on the outside to get me the white ones in a size twelve; but, the damn things were selling out of every store that had them on the east coast. Since one of my guys also needed to get a pair for him and his son, he traveled all the way to Washington D.C. and all he could find was the all black pair. Let's just say that I was the first brother rocking those in the system.

When my eyes started to go bad I told myself that there was no way in hell that I was gonna' be wearing some state issued glasses. After years of being in prison and being exposed to the bad lighting in this place, it can be bad for your eyes. So, when I found out that my people had the hookup at Kennedy & Perkins Eye Center on Whitney Avenue in downtown New Haven, my first order of business was to go hard with this chance opportunity so I copped several pairs of glasses starting with the Rose gold Gucci wireless frames strictly for the visits, the Nike flex-on frame were something to play in for work and the Ralph Lauren Polo frames were for at night when I was laying on the bunk reading in the cell to get my mind right before bed.

In prison you are only issued two tan uniforms. Under normal circumstances the average dudes would flex around the facility in one uniform and save one for a more special occasion like a visit or court trip. However, it was customary for me to find out who was working in the property room at every facility that I found myself in so that I could work out a way to at least have about five or six uniforms in my cell at any given time. One of the other things that I had to find out was who was working the laundry room so that I could get my contract in to start having my clothes done Chinese. This was important if you wanted to keep your whites looking new and fresh at all times. Chinese Laundry is when you commit to a verbal contract with one of the laundry workers to personally handle your laundry for you. The worker then personally washes your clothes with a little extra bleach, dries and folds them. He also presses your uniforms for you so that your shit stays tight. One thing you never want to do in prison is send your white off to the laundry and there is no one there to personally attend to your shit. Ten times out of ten your clothing will be returned to you looking like someone drug it through the mud. This comes by way of over packing the washing machines. Picture the clothes of over one hundred men being washed together at one time. Not only is that a small number that is some nasty shit waiting to happen!!! SMFH! Can you say body lice, boys and girls? LMMFAO!

If you didn't have a laundry connect, most brothers washed their clothing by hand either in the shower, the sink or in the toilet. Yeah, I said the toilet. You'd be surprised at how that cold water in a cleaned out toilet bowl can get the soap out of your cloths. True story, this is a practice that is picked up in the county jails and in hard times like solitary confinement I found myself using this method to keep my shit clean.

Lastly, hygiene should be everyone in prisons' top priority! Why? Because prison can be bad for your health, i.e., physically and mentally. Prison in and of itself is a nasty place for anybody to be. It is not the most well-kept environment to live in. a lot of those institutions are old and outdated; so, some have structural issues that are being overlooked by those in charge of our well-being. There exists a practice where the walls in every prison are just being painted over I'd say twice a year since these facilities have been open. No one has ever saw the need to strip the paint off the walls then paint on a new coat. There's problems with the plumbing systems due to the fact that they have these old lead pipes that over the years can become toxic causing the inmates to become sick or worse…die! The medical is not the best. At best, there are two Doctors to care for the medical needs of fourteen hundred prisoners. So, take a shower as often as you can and make sure that you invest time into keeping your cell clean. It is best to wash the floor of the cell using your hands. The mops are not the thing to use because they may have been shared with the other fifty cells in the unit. Always find a way to clean your toilet after every use. And after you take a piss, don't take a piece of dry tissue and smear the piss all over the toilet. That's not wiping the toilet clean. Get some soap and water and handle your business! Nobody wants to have to sit on top of your dry piss when they go to take a shit. -Smile!

### *My thoughts*

 *Coming to prison I was still caught up in this whole idea of wanting to have and maintain the image that I had on the street. Many men who were out on the streets getting money and then come to prison find themselves dealing with this identity crisis where we feel as though we need to still go the length to impress the next man. I am not saying that we need to walk the yard looking like bums. NO! I encourage you to always be natty and presentable. However, never put yourself at risk when at the end of the day no one really cares that you are caught up in selfish vanity!"*

# 9

# A CHANGE GONNA COME

This hustling shit in prison became like second *Nature* to me because it was all that I thought that I could do in life. I mean as a kid we all had aspirations of becoming something whether it was a fireman, postman, doctor and most of us even wanted to become a police officer as a kid. Yeah! I know most of the niggas reading this won't dear admit to ever possessing such a thought, especially now that you are in prison surrounded by a bunch of killers, robbers, rapist, thieves and the I don't fuck with the police types of motherfuckers. I GET IT! I REALLY DO! Smile!

Your secret's safe with me. I have literally been doing this shit since the age of twelve-years-old. Living life on the edge and putting my fucking freedom on the line for a few dollars. Although I made a fair amount of money behind these walls, I still found myself acquiring those same damn headaches that I got from motherfuckers when I was out in the free world. The only difference from being free when this took place and being in here locked up is that when I was free, I could escape the madness of it all by taking a ride down to New York or up to Massachusetts.

In prison there was no escaping the same fucking knuckle-heads who were either begging, borrowing or finding some way of fucking up what good things that they had left. So, whenever I felt this way I would stop going to the gym, or even the yard because there were times where I just didn't want to be bothered with the bullshit that came with being around a bunch of grown ass men all day. Hell! I wouldn't even go to the library and I was literally in a fight for my life; because, I knew that this would lead to me hearing something that I didn't want to be hearing at the moment. There was always somebody who was looking to get high and just didn't have the means at that time to afford it; so, they would always ask to be fronted some shit until they either got their state-pay, or in cash once their family member could send it or they were sitting on some old commissary that they thought I would except in exchange for some get high. I hated doing this because I only liked dealing with dudes who had their cash up front; but, I wasn't really in a position to take a chance on not giving a fiend his fix and running the risk of being set up by him.

So, I would just stay in my cell, lay on my bunk, listening to 94.3 WYBC and reminisce about all of the good times when I was home and the fun shit I use to do at an age where I should have had my bad ass in school in somebody's classroom getting an education. 94.3 WYBC, was known for playing the best variety of hits and oldies when it came to R&B music and it was sure to make any grown man cry at night just thinking about all the shit he's traded in for a two-man cell the size of a bathroom. Those love songs would have you thinking about all the pussy you no longer had access to. However, whenever I would lay on the bunk and the vibe was right, I would think about all of the fun I had and for some strange reason when I'd think of Harlem it just seemed to take my mind off of everything that was going on around me and all of the shit that I was going through.

I would think about how me and my so-called friends at the

time used to go to shows at the world famous Apollo Theater to see some of the top rappers in the game. Eric B. & Rakim, Big Daddy Kane, Kool G. Rap, Biz Markie, M.C. Shan, LL Cool J, KRS-ONE, Naughty by Nature and the entire Juice Crew All Stars. We'd make it our business to go to the Apollo Theater every Wednesday night just for Amateur night. We had a ritual where we would take care of whatever business needed to get taken care of before the evening; because, come 5:00pm we would be exiting the Getty gas station at the corner of Kimberly Avenue and Ella T. Grasso Boulevard to jump on the on ramp to Interstate-95 heading south. Ten Philly Blunts of Buddha rolled up which we chained smoked all the way down and this was repeated on the way back as well.

It only took us about an hour in total to reach our destination. However, we would leave this early so that we could do some shopping at Dr. Jays, A.J. Lester's Clothing or Blackman's Jewelers in the 125 MART on 125th Street. We would also go over to J&J Variety between 123rd Street and 7th Avenue so that we could get our hands on the latest Kid Capri mixtape to pump out of whatever car or truck we drove down that day. During this time there was no gentrification taking place in the borough of Harlem. This was a time before motherfuckers were duped into believing that Bill Clinton was the first black President just because his ass would frequent a local McDonalds in the hood and eat a Big Mac, large fries with a medium orange drink NO! ICE! SMH! Pun intended.

Sylvia's was one of the best soul food restaurants that I knew of on the east coast; besides Sandra's from around my hood, so I would slide through when I got the munchies from all that Buddha I was smoking. Another spot that I fell in love with was Shabazz on 116th Street and Lenox Avenue. This was that famous spot that is seen in the Spike Lee Joint "Malcolm X." were Denzel Washington hung out with the other brothers from the Fruit of Islam (F.O.I.). But, since this was a Muslim spot and

I was clearly on my bull shit, I had enough respect for those brothers not to go up in their establishment smelling like I was buried in weed smoke. However, they made a blazing steak & cheese sub on a wheat sub roll and my mother was especially fond of their bean pies. I never purchased a bean pie from the brothers that I would see standing on the street corners all dressed up in their natty suits and bow ties; however, I would always make it my business to bring a few bean pies home so that me and mom could do our thing. We would heat the pie up and top it off with a scoop of vanilla bean ice cream. I never thought that someone could make navy beans taste so damn good!

Of course I had my little shorty uptown that I would go and see from time to time. Her rest was located on 122nd Street and Manhattan Avenue directly across the street from the world's greatest entertainer Doug E. Fresh. She was a thick red bone sister that I loved spending time with because even though she was born and raised in the heart of Harlem, she was still green. Her mom and pops fucked with me hard to the point they would even let me stay the night if it was too late and I didn't want to take that drive back up Interstate-95 to Connecticut. I enjoyed their company because they smoked and I would stay up late puffing with her moms and talking about life. She was surprised at how young I was and the life that I was living amazed her.

I would even think about how I used to bring some young girls from around the way up top to cop some weight in coke and some weed. A lot of these girls had never left the town and had only heard of or seen New York on television. So it was exciting for someone like me to take them somewhere that they have never been before. Plus, I would treat them right in their eyes. I made it my business to always take them to Dr. Jays so that they could pick out a nice pair of Reebok sneakers in whatever color they chose. The rapper DMX said it best when he quoted in his song the lyrics "54/11 size seven in girls". He referred to the reeboks in this manner because they were priced at $54.11. So, this was nothing to a brother that was getting money during the early 1990's. During this time there were no White Castle burger joints in Connecticut; so, I would get off an exit in the Bronx just before Willis Street and the 3$^{rd}$ Avenue Bridge and let the young girl grab a few burgers and some cheese fries. She would nurse these chicken nugget size burgers all the way back home just so she could show off to her friends that she had been to New York. SMH! She never knew that when I went to put the bags in the trunk, those 54/11's held a half a kilo of cocaine at the bottom of the box that I needed to get back home with me safely.

The thing that I would use to fuck these young girls heads up was when I would call up my big brother Joey who had this bachelor pad on 122$^{nd}$ Street and Morningside Avenue right across the street from the Morningside Park. Several times I would make a quick stop at a pay phone and hit him up to tell him that I was coming through with company. Seeing that I was the little brother that he never had, it pleased him and he took pride in being able to look out for me like this. I would eventually drive over to the apartment and once we got inside they would be gassed up by how I moved about throughout the house as if it were mine. I was even given a room to stay in whenever I chose to impress a young girl like this. The apartment was laced with the best furniture money could buy; so, they thought they were spending the night at the W hotel. Not only that, they swore that I had a place of my own in Connecticut and New York. Once they got back to New Haven and shared this bit of information with the other girls around the way, they all were secretly vying to make the trip with me whenever I needed them to. They were even willing to go the extra mile to secure their spot in the passenger seat, if you know what I mean.

Besides having these sublime thoughts as I lay out on the bunk, I would think about some other fun times I spend visiting other cities and hustling in places like Baltimore, Maryland;

Springfield, Massachusetts; and Virginia Beach, Virginia. However, I was getting tired with my run on the system and was seriously considering my move away from all of the nonsense that was going on in and around my life. What did this change look like for me?

I had no idea; but I knew that a change was gonna come!

*"I've met many black geniuses who use their genius to navigate the penitentiary, which takes far more intelligence than it does to navigate even the most prestigious and powerful universities. If only they understood context and the importance of putting your skills to work in the right scenarios."*
*– Dr. Boyce Watkins, Financial Professor*

When I read statements like this being made by Scholars such as Dr. Boyce Watkins validating the great minds of black men in prison, it moves me to be the best example of a man that I can be whether behind these prison walls or out in the free world. I have always known my own self-worth; however, I just didn't want to put in the work to reach my full potential in life. See, each and every one of us are responsible for our own genius! Therefore, we must hold each other accountable for doing the right things at all times so that we are becoming a benefit to ourselves, our families, our families, our friends and our communities that we are to return to at some point in our lives.

### *My thoughts*

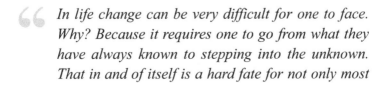
*In life change can be very difficult for one to face. Why? Because it requires one to go from what they have always known to stepping into the unknown. That in and of itself is a hard fate for not only most*

*men but women as well. This is why our country sees a national recidivism rate that is so high. Brothers don't want to change because they fear change and it is so much easier for them to go back to what they knew best. They say that the road to the Penitentiary (Hell) is paved with good intentions! Too often we find ourselves wanting to take the easy way out of any given situation that we may find ourselves in. If we would have only taken the hard roads in life, I can bet you that you'll enjoy the fruits of your labor a lot more. There are two things in life that pressure does, i.e. -it bust pipes and it also makes diamonds... so, strive to make a jewel out of your life situations!"*

# 10

# GROWTH AND DEVELOPMENT

When I first came to prison, religion was the furthest thing from my mind. I even thought that I was destined to hell for the man whose life that I had taken. I didn't necessarily grow up religious nor was I raised in a religious household – however - I was the son of a Panther. I even consider myself a Panther baby because my mother was an active member of the Black Panther Party when she gave birth to me on August 9, 1972. Let her tell it, that ten point program that all Panthers swore by was to be my religious way of life.

1. *We want freedom. We want power to determine the destiny of our Black community. We believe the Black people will not be free until we are able to determine our destiny.*
2. *We want full employment for our people. We believe that the federal government is responsible and obligated to give every man employment or a guaranteed income. We believe that if the white American businessmen will not give full employment, then the means of production should be taken from*

*the businessmen and placed in the community so that*
*the people of the community can organize and employ*
*all of its people and give a high standard of living.*

3. *We want an end to the robbery by the white man of*
   *our Black community. We believe that this racist*
   *government has robbed us and now we are*
   *demanding the overdue debt of forty acres and two*
   *mules. Forty acres and two mules was promised 100*
   *years ago as restitution for slave labor and mass*
   *murder of Black people. We will accept the payment*
   *in currency which will be distributed to our many*
   *communities. The Germans murdered six million*
   *Jews. The American racist has taken part in the*
   *slaughter of over fifty million Black people; therefore,*
   *we feel that this is a modest demand that we make.*

4. *We want decent housing, fit for shelter of human*
   *beings. We believe that if the white landlords will not*
   *give decent housing tour Black community, then the*
   *housing and the land should be made into*
   *cooperatives so that our community, with government*
   *aid, can build and make decent housing for its*
   *people.*

5. *We want education for our people that exposes the*
   *true nature of this decadent American society. We*
   *want education that teaches us our true history and*
   *our role in present-day society. We believe in an*
   *educational system that will give to our people a*
   *knowledge of self. If a man does not have knowledge*
   *of himself and his position in society and the world,*
   *then he has little chance to relate to anything else.*

6. *We want all Black men to be exempt from military*
   *service. We believe that Black people should not be*
   *forced to fight in the military service to defend a*
   *racist government that does not protect us. We will*

*not fight and kill other people of color in the world
who, like Black people, are being victimized by the by
the white racist government of America. We will
protect ourselves from the force and violence of the
racist police and the racist military, by whatever
means necessary.*

7.  *We want an immediate end to police brutality and
    murder of Black [people. We believe we can end
    police brutality in our Black community by
    organizing Black self-defense groups that are
    dedicated to defending our Black community from
    racist police oppression and brutality. The second
    amendment to the constitution of the United States
    gives a right to bear arms. We therefore believe that
    all Black people should arm themselves for self-
    defense.*

8.  *We want freedom for all Black men held in federal,
    state, county and city prisons and jails. We believe
    that all Black people should be released from the
    many jails and prisons because they have not
    received a fair and impartial trial.*

9.  *We want all Black people when brought to trial to be
    tried in court by a jury of their peer group or people
    from their Black communities, as defined by the
    constitution of the United States. We believe that the
    courts should follow the United States constitution so
    that Black people will receive fair trials. The
    Fourteenth Amendment of the US Constitution gives a
    man a right to be tried by his peer group. A peer is a
    person from a similar economic, social, religious,
    geographical, environmental, historical and racial
    background. To do this the court will be forced to
    select a jury from the Black community from which
    the Black defendant came. We have been and are*

*being tried by all-white juries that have no*
*understanding of the "average reasoning man" of the*
*Black community.*
10. *We want land, bread, housing, education, clothing,*
*justice and peace. And as our major political*
*objective, a United Nations-supervised plebiscite to*
*be held throughout the Black colony in which only*
*Black colonial subjects will be allowed to participate,*
*for the purpose of determining the will of Black*
*people as to their national destiny. Etc.*

My mom was quick to let it be known that the white man (or pig as they called him) that hung on most walls in the homes in Black America, could never be her God. This is what she would say to me! My mother knew early on that the picture of Jesus on the peoples' walls was nothing but a depiction of the famous painter Michael Angelo's cousin. My mother was a very conscious woman in that sense!

Then again there was no way I could get away with talking that black power movement shit in grandmother's house. My grandmother loved everybody as the church had instructed her to do so. This was my father's mother and she had literally grew up in the church. At the age of thirteen her grandfather and father were heavy into their religion so much so they started a church in New Haven named Thomas Chapel. There's even a room named after my great grandfather in the church, it's Lloyd Taylor something. The church was originally founded on Webster Street near Dixwell Avenue in New Haven. However, over the years and due to the influx of cash that came in from people who probably could not afford to part with the money that they gave up weekly as offerings, the church would move into its new location on Dixwell Avenue near Argyle Street.

As a child I can vaguely remember going to church by force of course. Truthfully speaking, children should not be made to go to church until they can be willing participants in this shit. Because no child should be made to sit still for that long and subject to an ass whooping' if they get tired and start moving all around the fucking church. That shit can be a form of child abuse. Especially if you got one of those holy rollers in your family that volunteers to take you to Bible study on Tuesday, Choir practice on Wednesday, Revival on Friday and both morning and afternoon services on Sunday because they done decided to go and catch the damn holy ghost! SMH!

The one thing I did like about church is the fact that the building was nice and there were always some other bad ass kids for me to play and share in getting an ass whooping' with. No one even took the time to tell me that there was a protocol for one attending this place of worship. And what the fuck was behaving anyway? I damn sure didn't have an idea at the age of five, six, or even seven years old for that matter! So, parents strive to give your children an understanding of what you expect from them when you are putting them in this situation because this type of pressure can easily make a child resent the church.

It was because of this reason, I was resentful and never felt the need to go to church when I first came to prison. Brothers that I was dealing with would always ask me to come down to church service to hang out and talk with them. This is when I had come to find out that church in prison was like a bar or club in the streets. It was the place where people went for social gathering. It was crazy because it was as if every crook, robber, rapist, thief, murderer, and gangbanger had found their god on the inside. The place looked more like hell if you'd ask me! It became a form of out of cell time because the prison was only letting you out of the cells but so many hours a day. So, convicts (which I am not) saw this as a way of creating more recreation (out-of-cell) time for themselves.

When I would show up to these services, I never felt comfortable in this space. One of the reason was because of the traumas associated with all of those ass whippings I had to relive and I always possessed somewhat of an innate ability to be respectful towards people, and their places of worship. But now I sit in their space passing drugs off to the next man, having gang meetings, passing kites (prison letters) to other gang members giving them orders on what needs to get done in their blocks, and all the other shit that goes against the prison rules. I would also be expose to seeing some shit that I wasn't used to seeing and I always found it to be a bit disturbing to me. It's a fucked up sight to see a man I once knew or even thought I knew hugged up with a homosexual in the same manner that I would see him out on the streets with his Childs mother. It is clear to me that these brothers have lost their minds. This shit was all new to me. I mean I can empathize with a man getting a life sentence because I was serving a virtual life sentence myself. However, I cannot nor will I ever consider empathizing with a man who thinks that just because he'll never in his life get another piece of pussy that he can substitute that with another grown mans' asshole! That's just not gonna happen! Not in a million years! This is the ultimate sign of weakness in a man behind these walls and these fools are always the ones that are quick to demand that they be respected. How in the fuck can a 'man' let his moral compass go that far to the left? Man PLEASE! Beat your dick. I mean people are gonna be who they are going to be, point blank. I get it! I don't hate an individual that choses to live this life because at the end of the day it is his life; however, I am against the proliferation of homosexuality in the black community. Especially in the penitentiary. It's just a cop-out.

Being that there is only but so much one man can take and the distaste this shit brought to me after seeing this, I chose to spend my time elsewhere amongst some righteous folk. A lot of other brothers had come to share in my sentiment in this regard; so, we all started attending the Black Muslim services. This took place for me with my arrival to the Somers Correctional Institution in Somers, Connecticut. During this time the Nation of Islam had a strong hold on the Connecticut prison system and was not to be fucked with. Orthodox Islam was pretty much nonexistent back then. I mean not one beard in sight...

When I arrived at Somers, I had no idea what the fuck a Nation of Islam was nor have I ever heard of some Fruit of Islam! My first thought was that some Figs or some other fruit was coming from the Middle East and into the prison. But, in time I had come to get to know brothers who held names like Floyd X., Fred X., James X., Darryl X. (Barkim), David X., and George X. (Cuban George). The F.O.I. were some serious brothers. They moved with and demonstrated a sense of militancy that I have never witnessed before in the world nor in prison. They were some highly disciplined individuals.

Brothers Floyd, Fred and George X. are the brothers that I found myself gravitating towards. Whenever I was in their presence, these brothers were always speaking truth to power – as they would say. When I would go up in their service the things they were building on and talking about spoke directly to the core of my being. They were building on the plight of the Blackman here in the Wilderness of North America, especially the black men that sat in this physical hell! They were breaking down the 13$^{th}$ Amendment in the United States Constitution way before I fully understood what they were actually stating to their core audience. Mentioning things like, 'Blackman, because we committed the crimes that we are here for we allowed this system to usher us right back into the shackles and chains that they said they freed us from'. This was some profound shit and it resonated with me because I was just as angry as any other black man that was being enslaved by this racist system. See, whenever a young black man is sent off to prison for the rest of his life, he has this anger towards not just the criminal justice system but every white man and woman; be it the police officer, lawyer, prosecutor, or judge, even the Correctional Officers who they feel had a hand in putting them here in the first place. The rise in the American prison system is by design. Think I'm lying? Just read *"The New Jim Crow, by Michelle Alexander"*. There are over 2.2 million people in the American prison system. This country has more prisoners than any country in the world! There are more black men in prison today then there were in slavery in 1850! So, prison by design was a way of stifling the rise of the Blackman here in America.

When I got to Somers, everybody was telling me to sign up for December fast. I did not know what these dudes were telling me to do; that is, until George X. approached me in the main hall one day and told me that I should come down to December fast and I asked him what was this December fast that everyone is talking about? George X. was a tall brown skin brother who had come to the country during the exodus from Fidel Castro's Cuba. He sought refuge in New York upon his arrival, then landed in New Haven and ultimately the state's prison system. He explained to me that the December fast was something the Nation of Islam did every December. Not taking what he had shared with me at face value, I dug in a little further with the questioning as to why (?) without wanting to offend him. He told me that Master Fard Muhammad (PBUH) who is the founder of the Nation of Islam and his Minister the Honorable Elijah Muhammad (PBUH), thought that the Black man and women here in the United States of America should have their own. He would go on to mentioned that blacks in America spend more money than any other race of people in America during the Thanksgiving holiday and especially during Christmas time, and the fasting that took place during the month of December wasn't just about something physical and spiritual. It was about having discipline when it came to blacks being the consumers of corporate America and making everyone else rich off of our backs and hard labors.

*"I was aware of the brother Malcolm X. (Hon. El-Hajj Malik*

*El-Shabazz) because I would see picture of him as a kid. Plus,
whenever I would go to New York City, I would drive down
Malcolm X. Boulevard; however, I never bothered to get into
who this man was nor did I care at this time."*

But, all of what brother George was saying to me made a hell
of a lot of sense because I bore witness to the struggles of my
mother and father at these times when they wanted their children
to have all of these presents at Christmas time and they were
even willing to miss paying the rent so that we would be happy
for this one day and then we would literally be fucked for the
next six months trying to recoup. WTF! I assured George that I
would sign up for December fast but I had just got about twenty
pepperoni sticks in with my Christmas package and I was not
throwing them away. Yeaah! Damn it! I was wining and dining,
smoking and drinking. I was with the bullshit still, give me some
credit would you!

Brother Fred X., was the first brother to give me a hand
written copy of the '*Student Enrollment*' which is the first lesson
a Muslim gets after going through the Nation of Islam's Orienta-
tion packet. My reading at this time was very poor so I didn't
bother reading it at all and there was no way I was going to
expose the fact that I could not read to some brothers that I had
just met. I didn't trust people that easy because I had trust issues
way before I came to prison. Prison just compounded my issues
and made them worse than I could ever imagine. Anyway, I held
onto this hand written copy of the student enrollment for about
ten years before I got rid of it or lost it in transfer. The Orienta-
tion packet was interesting because it showed you how to write
the Nation of Islam headquarters in Chicago Illinois and request
that as a member you be given your X…

Shit, I had a hard time spelling Connecticut; so, I knew right
then and there that I wasn't writing no Chicago to receive no X.
from the Honorable Minister Louis Farrakhan.

Brother Floyd X., impacted my life a great deal and got me

into writing. I could relate to Brother Floyd because I found myself similarly situated with regards to him and me both having caught our cases at the age of seventeen years old and the possibility that we would basically be living out the rest of our days behind bars. He was from Hartford Connecticut and most if not all of the brothers from Hartford at this time were a part of a gang called the 20 Love; but, Floyd was willing to stand on his own and in his faith. Upon my arrival to Somers prison, the brother had been incarcerated for a decade and was serving a sentence of eighty-years! What fucking medieval superior court prosecutor and judge felt comfortable with sentencing a seventeen-year-old child to so much damn time in an adult prison is beyond me! Does anyone ever sit and consider the trauma that must be associated with that? I'm just saying, damn!

I can remember when I became a subscriber of the Final Call Newspaper that is the national newspaper of the Nation of Islam. The Final Call covered a wide range of news from all over the world and the centerfold was always a space specifically reserved for an article by Minister Farrakhan. These articles were some of the best things that I had ever come to read in my life and because I was coming into this new and exciting information I could not wait to share what I had read with others in my cipher. So, I would run to the yard and give the papers to one of the brothers so that they could read what Farrakhan had written and break it down for me due to the fact that they were studying these life-saving teachings under the guidance of the Most Honorable Minister Louis Farrakhan.

Unbeknownst to me Floyd X. had an eye on me and questioned me one day as to whether or not I was in fact reading the papers that I have been getting. I told him that I was in fact reading the papers. With that statement asserted by me, Floyd requested that from this day on I bring out a 200-words essay on the centerfold. Remember that I was far from a writer at this time. However, I knew that I had to start somewhere and this led to me having to write a 200-word essay each and every week. Let's just say that I am pleased with how far I have come in the field of writing. Hey! I'm penning this book right now.

A few years would pass by and the prison (Somers) was closing its doors and would no longer be holding maximum security inmates. In the late 1980's and early 1990's, the State of Connecticut had just invested hundreds of millions of dollars into the construction of several new prisons built to complement the rise and boom in mass-incarceration that was taking place throughout the United States of America! There were several prisons that had been built and were being opened during the early 90's. You had the newly built Walker Reception Center which would be receiving all inmates being sentenced from throughout the state; Gardner Correctional Institute in Newtown, Connecticut – a town that would go on to become famous after Adam Lanza thought it would be the right thing to do when he murdered his mother, then went into an elementary school and killed teachers and children on December 14, 2012; Corrigan Correctional Center out towards the New London Turnpike; and the infamous MacDougall Correctional Institution in Suffield, Connecticut.

When Somers Prison was going through its transition, just about ninety percent of its population was transferred to the MacDougall Correctional Institution in Suffield, Connecticut. MacDougall, would come to be known as Sweet Dougall because it had become infamous for housing some of the states' wealthiest inmates there. Individuals like convicted Rapist Alex Kelly, Richard "wood chipper" Craft who murdered his wife and chopped her body up using a wood chipper and of course Michael Skakel who was tried and convicted of the murder of Martha Moxley and later cleared on all charges.

Arriving at MacDougall was like going from the slums to the suburbs. On January 7, 1994 I was one of the first two-hundred or so prisoners to be transferred to this new facility in Suffield

Connecticut. Since inmates were being transferred out of the prison and into this new facility, the Department of Correction had their own plan in mind as well. The Nation of Islam was too radical for them and in no way did they want to run the risk of having forty or fifty brothers being housed in their new facility operating under the guise of a small army with Captain, Lieutenants and private Soldiers...this was not happening! So, when the new facility was opening the powers that be saw the need to hire Muslim Chaplains who were Sunni Muslims in the order of the orthodox Islam faith as taught by the Prophet Muhammad (PBUH) 1,400 years ago.

Over the years you would see the minds of some great men being transformed into a more docile and meek individual. Gone was that sense of militancy that I was drawn to and their Fez headwear was being traded in for a Kufi. I went from seeing a group of men being perpendicular and praying upright to bending at the knees and making prostration. Brothers no longer spoke about attending December fast but they began to watch the lunar calendar to see when the crescent moon was coming in for the holy month of Ramadan. There were no more lead Ministers in the facility for the brothers but instead a facility Imam. They weren't even calling each other brother any more, instead they were referring to each other as Ock! I saw languages go from English to Quranic Arabic overnight! Within a years' time I witnessed a Nation of Men be reduced to a bunch of beard wearing Saudi Prince Wannabes'. Seeing this shift in cultural world views in a matter of no time left my mind wondering what the fuck is happening before me. I had a lot of unanswered questions in my head that needed to be answered. I often wondered how a man could go from telling me that "*The Original man is the Asiatic Blackman, the maker, owner, cream of the planet earth, father of civilization God of the universe!*"- To now not knowing his own fucking origin in this world? If you ask me, that's some straight savage shit…a savage is a person who has lost the knowledge of himself!

### *My thoughts*

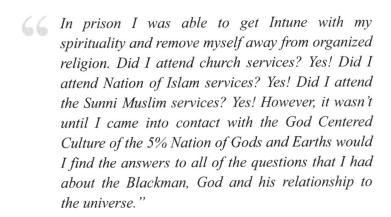

> *In prison I was able to get Intune with my spirituality and remove myself away from organized religion. Did I attend church services? Yes! Did I attend Nation of Islam services? Yes! Did I attend the Sunni Muslim services? Yes! However, it wasn't until I came into contact with the God Centered Culture of the 5% Nation of Gods and Earths would I find the answers to all of the questions that I had about the Blackman, God and his relationship to the universe."*

# 11

# GOOD ORDERLY DIRECTION

My answers to all of the above would come from my mental father who taught me the Knowledge of myself, as well as my origin in this world. For that praise will always be due! I had the pleasure of meeting this brother named "Black" out in the free world when I was home and with the bullshit. His first cousins and I were cool. We had met in middle school when they moved to New Haven from Coney Island, New York. Later on Blacks sister Sandy and my sister Michelle would become good friends and hang out and club a lot. Black and his teenage cousins would go on to become a fixture in the drug trade in the City of New Haven. And as always wherever you can find someone getting money off of drugs, you can expect violence to follow behind all of the money you are getting. Black had caught a manslaughter beef in the early 90's and he and I would end up coming into contact with each other when we got to MacDougall. We were being housed in the same unit and since we had known each other from the streets we both agreed that we should share a cell together.

When Black and I moved into the cell together, I noticed that he had some ways about him that were different. His mannerism was somewhat like those that I saw in brothers from the Nation of Islam and he always was greeting the other prisoners with Peace! So, one day I had asked him if he was N.O.I. and his response was "Nah! I'm Five Percent."

Now the Five Percenters were something that I was a little familiar with for several reason. When I would go to the Apollo Theater in Harlem I would always have to drive pass this burnt out old building at the corner of 126$^{st}$ and 7$^{th}$ Avenue which I'd later come to find out is the headquarters for the 5% Nation of Gods and Earths. I can also remember in the early 1980's my older brother King Bee would go to New York and always return with these fly ass Kufis' with the tassel on them. I knew that he and his friends were into something. Another reason was due to the Hip-Hop scene. You had Rakim from the rap group Eric B. & Rakim. Groups like Brand Nubian was one of my favorites. Especially their album One for All. Not to mention my sister had her first child by Big Daddy Kane. I use to wonder what his name stood for when I first met him but never really asked. Then I heard him break it down in one of his song..." The name Kane is superior to many people, it means <u>K</u>ing, <u>A</u>siatic, <u>N</u>obody <u>E</u>qual!" When I was first able to comprehend that I was like oh! Shit! Kane is nice as hell when it comes to rappin'. Kane and my sister named their son Lamel and I am sure that his name has some esoteric science behind it that I don't know yet.

Then came the Wu-Tang Clan to put a hurting on the rap game. You had nine Gods all in one group doing their thing. "*<u>C</u>ash <u>R</u>ules <u>E</u>verything <u>A</u>round <u>M</u>e, CREAM get the money dolla dolla bill ya'll!*" I can go on and on about them; but, if you want to know who they are for yourself just check out their documentary "Mics and Men".

Although I knew of these rappers that were a part of the Nation of Gods and Earths; who are commonly known as the Five Percenters, I knew little to nothing about what this way of life was about or anything that they taught other then everyone saying peace to one another. So, I had asked Black to tell me what the 5%ers were about and he went right into it at God speed. He first made it known to me what the Nation of Gods and Earths teach.

*"We teach that Black people are the original people of the planet earth."*

*"We teach that Black people are the fathers and mothers of civilization."*

*"We teach that the science of supreme mathematics is the key to understanding man's relationship to the universe."*

*"We teach that Islam is a natural way of life and not a religion."*

*"We teach that education should be fashioned to enable us to be self-sufficient as a people."*

*"We teach that each one should teach one according to their knowledge."*

*"We teach that the Blackman is god and his proper name is ALLAH: Arm Leg, Leg, Arm, Head."*

*"We teach that our children are our link to the future and they must be nurtured, respected, loved, protected and educated."*

*"We teach that the unified Black family is the vital building block of the nation."*

Allah Blackness was spitting this shit off of his tongue rapid speed and he had my fucking head spinning. He had committed all of this to memory. He further built on the Blackman is the original inhabitant of the planet earth and how the Blackman was created in the image and likeness of God on a mental and physical level. He took me to the bible and pointed out things to me that were evident but I had never been made aware of them by anyone that I knew who considered themselves to be at all religious.

Some of the other things he showed me in the scripture just made absolute sense to me and I hold those truths to this day. The God would manifest to me that the Blackman was made in the image and likeness of God. He grabbed his bible and turned to Genesis handed me the *"good book"* and had me read from chapter one, verses 26 through 27 and as I read '& God said, let *US* make man in *OUR* image, after *OUR* likeness...so God created man in his *OWN* image, in the image of God created he him.' Then he broke down to me that the word God is a noun and nouns are used to describe people, places, and things; so, the devil was trying to deceive the original people by trying to get them to believe that they were not Gods but little gods. Then the brother asked me who God was talking to when he stated in verse 26 "let 'US' make man in 'OUR' image, after 'OUR' likeness?

Allah Blackness, didn't even allow me to answer him. He just went right into letting me know that there were already people here. Then he told me to go to Genesis five where it states God created man in the image of him, and in the image of him, he made them and called *'their'* name ADAM! At this very moment in time, the God was showing and proving to me that Adam wasn't one person but in fact a group of people according to the epistle. – read the shit for yourself if you don't believe this truth that I am manifesting to you on these pages! The God was bombing me with scripture...Exodus 7:1; Luke 17:20 & 21; John 10:34 & 35; Habakkuk 3:3, etc. I guess he may have thought that I had a Christian upbringing so he saw a need to bombard me with 'the word.'

I always felt that I was one with some sense and to this point, this is one of the reasons I chose to stay away from and never read the bible or any religious text for that matter. I knew that whatever I was to read in these books and they held some weight, I would then have to be responsible for living it out to the best of my ability. This became a challenge for me because I was coming from a life of savagery into my God consciousness and as a child we all have an innate ability to know right from wrong.

Back in 1994, I got the knowledge of self from Allah Blackness; however, I thought that being God meant that I could just do whatever the fuck I wanted to and that is exactly what I did. Yeah! I was feeling myself and my ego and pride was getting the best of me at this time. Then several years would pass by before I would learn more about the Nation and what it meant for me to be a poor righteous teacher. Once these moral principles were laid out for me I began to live them out to the best of my ability.

I went from allowing others to call me "Ray Dog" as I was known on the streets to the name that my enlightener would call me. Looking back, I guess one could say that I was a beast out on those streets and somewhat savage in the pursuit of what happiness I was getting from the life. The God would call me Ray Cee and the Cee is the third alphabet in the Supreme Alphabets -Cee/See- means to Cee with the third eye which is the mind and See is with your two physical eyes which are the doorways to your third eye. Whenever Allah Blackness and I would build, he would always admire me for my level of understanding. As he taught me the lessons, he would make sure that I had a proper understanding of what he was conveying to me.

One day I was building with the brother about the double-mindedness of man and the great decisive battle going on in the minds of men such as myself every day as we strive to bring about transformation in our lives and how it can be related directly to the story in the book of Revelations 12:7, where it speaks about "& there was a war in heaven:" and I went into breaking this down for the brother so that we could see eye-to-eye on the matter. I remember telling him to 'see heaven as the mind and the angels being positive thoughts and the dragon being negative thought in the mind as it is read in the context of the scripture. In other words, the mind can be heaven or hell given the thoughts that it is manifesting at any given moment in time! The mind is the highest elevation of man. The mind is the place where great battles are fought. Heaven and hell exist within the mind of man. Heaven is what you make it and hell is what you go through. For if you surely love God (& it is who you be) you will go through hell, to see to it that you come out right and exact. To do this Blackman, you must be a savior of self, meaning you must begin to manifest "the spirit of man" to work, labor, and toil the knowledge, wisdom, and understanding of who you be. And you be God! -in the physical and not some spook in the sky.

I fought this decisive battle, and won. Now I was living by this notion of "**What would God do?**" when it came to living out the manifestation of my words, ways and actions on a daily basis. As the late great Dr. Frances Cress Welsing once said, "*We are the mothers and fathers of the earth.*" So, all we as Black men have to do is tap into our God given potential and deal with self-realization and self-actualization on a physical plane.

Did this happen overnight for me? Of course not! I literally had to go through hell in order to come out right in this situation. You know how the bible talks about a "double minded man being unstable in all his ways"? Well, I was in fact that man...I still had my mind in the streets and I was battling with doing the right things in life. Was this hard for me to do? Emphatically yes! But, I loved myself enough to do what I needed to for me to be the God conscious man that I am today. I had to go inside of myself and literally cure myself of the disease (dis-ease) of crime and a criminal way of thinking. It's as if I was tasked with gutting out an old house and rebuilding it all by myself. So, I had started by going into rooms that I had never entered since my childhood and throwing shit out that I had been holding on to for far too long. I had to go up into my attic (mind) and get rid of ideologies that I was living by that were bringing me nothing but harm. I had to go from thinking animalistic as 'Ray dog' to thinking as the God Ra'Sun Allah! I had to flip that dog around to God.

This came with much resistance from the Connecticut Department of Correction. I had to face down this Administration that was refusing to allow me to live out my God Centered Culture. Yeah! They did not want hundreds of Black men running around their prison "Believing" that they were gods. Can you imagine the fear this must have struck into the lives of these white folks that had no understanding of what the Nation of Gods and Earths was about? They were trying to stop the growth and development of the Supreme Being Blackman at all cost. They went around taking brothers' lessons and threatening to place brothers in long term Administrative Segregation for teaching their truth in the facility. This administration was even going so far as labeling brothers mentally insane because they were chosen to live out this way of life. Having their mental health levels raised because they were saying that they were Gods! But yet and still if you were to pose the question to any of these people placing these false labels upon us to name one Greek god and the first proud thing to come out of their mouths is...Zeus! But, the Blackman can't be God? Fool! SMFH!

Being who I be...God! I didn't run from them nor their threats of being labeled a disruptive group or possibly a gang. And these devils were doing their best to hang the gang label on us. Fear was presented to me as *False Evidence Appearing Real*; so, not being afraid I went up against this Department of Corruption and stood on my square against the Attorney General with his Army of Attorneys'. I ran all their asses directly through the doors of the United States' Federal Court for the District of Connecticut in Hartford and sued the shit out of them! The Gods will always tell you anything that you *love*, you gotta go through *hell* to see it come out *right*!

In 2007, I was transferred from Cheshire Correctional Institute back to MacDougall Correctional Institute where there were several Gods who always stood for what the culture was about and always dealt with me on the level of equality even when I was with the bullshit, hustling and nonsense. Upon my arrival these brothers were building with me and telling me how the administration was coming after the lessons and trying to say that our God Centered Culture was being related to gangs and gang violence in the prison. They did confiscate some lessons from some brothers that they labeled Latin Kings, Bloods or Crip gang members. This left a bad taste in my mouth because for one there were some associated with gangs that were trying to use the language of the five percenters to shield their way of life within their dysfunctional families. I was once a gang member so if anyone knows, I know firsthand what it means to go from Devilishment (gang member) to Righteousness (God). It is such a beautiful thing – Word is bond!

We built on who is the best knower however, when it came to seeing to it the Gods had their own within the system. After several tedious meetings in the law library between myself and the Gods who attended, it was agreed upon that I would take the lead on seeking our rights from the Department of Correction so that the Five Percent Nation of Gods and Earths would be able to live out our culture free from the oppression that they had begun to place on our necks.

The Connecticut Department of Correction had placed a blanket ban on all things associated with the Nation of Gods and Earths. The security division captains, lieutenants, and officers had waged an all-out war on the gods – taking their lessons, plus degrees, books, and any periodical that they could get their hands on; like the Five Percenter Newspaper, the Light of the Sun, and the Sun of Man, to ensure that the Black man's claim to their Godhood was nonexistent! Several Gods were not being affected by these actions. I was never worried about the threat that was being sent my way; because, I have always known a threat to be a universal sign of weakness. So, they were actually giving me the sign that I was looking for. I held a lions' position and they were the wounded gazelle; so, Godspeed I was all over their ass and not letting up on them.

I can remember one day I was in the library where they keep their lies buried studying some case law when an officer came into the library and told me to gather up my stuff because he was given orders to come get me and escort me to the Warden's office as soon as possible. Again I knew my position. Normally when an officer is sent to get you and escort you to the Warden's office, shit is about to get ugly!!! That wasn't the case for me; however, I walked to the Wardens office poised and perpendicular and on my square. Unbeknownst to the Administration days earlier I had received a shit load of case law from other Federal District Courts throughout the United States' detailing how those District Courts were handling their states'; so, I was ready for war and in my hands I held the gun with a hundred round clip.

I walked into the office and was immediately surrounded by the entire security division for the facility...a scare tactic that I was way too familiar with from my days as a gang member. The Deputy Warden sat behind the Wardens desk and out of my peripheral I could see this fucking chump peering over at the phone which led me to believe that the Director of Security was on the line tuning in to the conversation. Keeping a short story short, they were threatening me about how South Carolina has the Gods affiliated as a gang and how they are in long term segregation and whether or not I want to risk being placed under the same situation?

In my head, I'm like BITCH! You know good damn and well that you can't do shit to me or else you would have just put my black ass in the gang unit. At this time the gang unit was on a decline and the only gangs that they were dealing with were mostly the Bloods and Crips. A lot of the old gangs in the system were pretty much nonexistent so they needed to fill up those beds to keep these units open. With the threat of labeling the Gods a gang, I reached into my legal work and pulled out a case that just came out in the State of Illinois, where a Federal Judge ordered all of the Gods be released into the general population units and issued identification other than their gang unit I.D.'s. Furthermore, I encouraged them all to make a Xerox copy for themselves to keep because this is what they were looking forward to being up against in the very near future if they kept fucking with me and the Gods; whether they like it or not, we were going to win.

This case rocked their foundation for the very simple fact that it dealt with the removal of the gang label from the Gods and placing these brothers back into the general population setting where which was their rightful place as they served out their time in a righteous way. All across the nation these district courts were finding these so-called correctional institutions were violating our First Amendment Rights and the Religious Land Use and Institutionalized Persons Act (RLUIPA) of 2000, by classifying the Nation of Gods and Earths as a security group or disruptive group. If you were to google cases won by the Nation of Gods and Earths, you will see that we are kicking their asses in the court of law and having our own legitimate path to god recognized.

I had accumulated so much paperwork on the Department of Correction before initially filing the 1983 civil suit that by the time I filed it they must have thought I was just bluffing and stock piling paper. However, when the time did come to take my position they didn't have a leg to stand on in the court of law. I battled them and beat them on their filing of a motion to dismiss my claims. Once this was done I was able to be appointed pro-bono legal counsel to assist me in fighting the case. Since this was never about coming up financially, there was never going to be a settlement where they would be able to throw me a few thousand dollars and it would silently all go away. Emphatically NO! That wasn't going to happen.

I'm pretty sure that they thought that they would wear me out and I would just give up because they may have been going off of the person they had only come to know on paper. However, it was clear that they had no fucking idea of the man that I had become since my arrival to prison. Gone was the seventh grade dropout who was reading on a fourth grade level; because, I had elevated my mental growth and development and was like Sampson ready to slay Goliath!!!

The Federal Magistrate had scheduled a trial date for June 13, 2016 and we were ready to show up and show and prove. I even had the lawyers going crazy about the date because they were stating to me that June 13th was a special day for the Nation of Gods and Earths. That it was…it was actually the day Show & Prove. An honor day where sincere adherents to the Nation of Gods and Earths Honor Father Allah (PBUH) on the day that he was assassinated (June 13, 1969). However, just two weeks before the set date I was sitting at my desk, in front of the computer doing my work as a clerk in the kitchen when the head supervisor received a call with someone on the other end of the line telling him to send me back to the housing unit for an urgent legal phone call. So, I headed back to the unit and just as I was approaching the unit my counselor was waiting outside of the block and asked that I follow her. She walked me into the Unit Managers office to make the call. As soon as my attorneys' got on the phone I was wondering to myself "what the fuck done happen now?!" However, they were calling me to inform me that the Connecticut Department of Correction did not want to move forward with a trial. In my mind I was saying "All praise is due to me!" for making this possible and the Gods within my cipher for trusting in me and seeing that I was the one being of the said ability to fight this battle for us.

The lawyers made it clear to me that if I wanted to go to trial and reject the states' offer they were ready to go and they were sure we would win and be paid heavily. However, I made it clear to them this fight has never been about winning in the form of some monetary value. I could give two fucks about the money I stood to win from these jackasses. The state sits aside money every year just for shit like this. My fight was strictly about principle, nothing more nothing less! I needed to show the devil that he/she was wrong in how it was depicting the Gods and I did just that. One of the most humbling outcome of this whole situation was when I came face to face with the old Director of Security who had now became the Warden at the facility the I was in and how she pulled me to the side and said to me:

*"Ra'Sun I hope that we can let bygones be bygones and move forward from this and I need you to see and understand that I was only working in the capacity that my position would allow me to work in."*

I respected her fine ass for coming to me like a woman. Hellme and several of the brothers even awarded her with a personal plaque for her service to the Department of Correction when she retired as Warden from the Osborn Correctional Institute back in 2017.

In May of 2016, the Connecticut Department of Correction entered into a settlement agreement with me which ordered them to remove the Nation of Gods and Earths from their security risk group "disruptive group listing". This false label was put on us because they could never – nor will they ever – establish a structure of hierarchy amongst the Gods. Stupid! This is because each and every God is the sole controller of his own universe (Life) and life simply means *L*ive *I*slamically *F*or *E*ver! Basically one is to live peacefully forever...and you don't need no one governing you on living out a right and just life.

Currently, all sincere adherents to the tenets of the Nation of Gods and Earths are able to live out this culture freely within the confines of the Connecticut Department of Correction. Are they happy about having to settle? No! But, fuck'em! Because as Father Allah (PBUH) would say the devil gets his man and Gods get his and their arms were too short to box with God. I live out my culture each and every day in each and every way I possibly can on this plantation.

### *My thoughts*

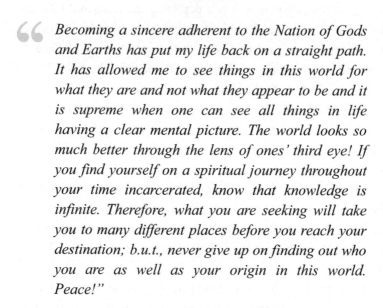

*Becoming a sincere adherent to the Nation of Gods and Earths has put my life back on a straight path. It has allowed me to see things in this world for what they are and not what they appear to be and it is supreme when one can see all things in life having a clear mental picture. The world looks so much better through the lens of ones' third eye! If you find yourself on a spiritual journey throughout your time incarcerated, know that knowledge is infinite. Therefore, what you are seeking will take you to many different places before you reach your destination; b.u.t., never give up on finding out who you are as well as your origin in this world. Peace!"*

# 12

## LIKE MINDEDNESS

In early January 2013, while I was at MacDougall Correctional Institute I had come out of the housing unit that I was being housed in in L-pod heading towards medical and as I got to the door, the Warden and I would come face-to-face. We weren't on speaking terms because he was in his feelings about being sued in the Nation of Gods and Earths case but as our paths crossed he just looked at me and asked "so, when is it going to happen?" I had no idea what he was talking about; so, I turned to him and responded by asking "when is what happening?" the Warden said to me, aren't you up for a level reduction? Because, I want you out of my facility! This was all news to me and out of the sixteen or so hundred prisoners in this facility he was overzealous about knowing when my level was scheduled to be reduced and wanting me out of the facility. As this exchange was going on, he reached for his I-Phone and went at typing something into it. I stood there in somewhat of amazement when he turned to me and told me that my level was up for reduction and he was signing off on it and that he would be sending one of his Captains by to see me so that I could tell him which level three facility I wanted to be transferred to.

The Captain came to see me and informed me the Warden wanted me to provide him with two facilities that I would want to go to when I was transferred. My first option was the Enfield Correctional Institute in Enfield Connecticut. Word was continuously making its way back to me from my A-alikes that this was one of the best places for me if I had to do time. It had little amenities as it relates to the recreation, the housing situation, and the ability to go outdoors and get fresh air...which is pretty much non-existent in level four facilities. The air is always recycled and you only get outside recreation from late April through late September. If the weather is bad you can forget about recreation altogether! I needed the fresh air badly after breathing in the recycled air for the past twenty-one years. Plus, I wanted to get back in tune with nature as much as I possibly could. I wanted to hear the Wind blow, the Birds chirp, run my fingers through the Grass and open my window whenever I wanted to and just listen to the rain as it cascaded down from the heavens. I also put in to go to Radgowski Correctional Institute out in Uncasville, Connecticut. As that old adage goes, 'you never miss a good thing until it's gone!' I was in dire need of getting back with the elements of the Sun, Rain hail and Snow...this was actually a sign that I was a step closer to being free.

On February 2, 2013, my level was reduced from a level four to a level three which means that I would be officially awaiting transfer to a medium security prison. The Warden would come and pay me another visit. However, this time his approach was a little off; because, as he neared me he stated that he had some good news and some bad news and asked, which one did I want to hear first? Assuming that he had reneged on my level reduction; I told him that I want to hear the bad news first...so, he informed me that I would not be going to either of the facilities that I had chosen. He further said that Osborn Correctional Institute was the only facility willing to accept me and had they not accepted me, he would have exercised his power of putting me in one of his level three units where my movement would be restricted. But, he did not want me in his prison and it would be best for the both of us if I left.

On Friday, March 8, 2013 the weather was bad and the state was experiencing a winter snow storm. Usually, transfers are not done during storms and the Governor would order that all roads be shut down; but, I guess this Warden really wanted me out of 'his' facility! So, I was transferred to the Osborn Correctional Institution (formally the infamous/notorious Somers Correctional Institution). I went through the admittance process which was funny as all hell. When I went into the property room in G-Basement, several brothers I had been doing time with were working as A/P workers and these brothers had informed him that I had been the talk of the day and the entire Administration was awaiting my arrival. There was a lot of talk amongst individuals about what type of problem I would be and how they planned on dealing with this problem (me). This was funny because it was coming from a group of people who had no idea whatsoever about who I was. I shrugged it off, grabbed my things and waited for an Officer's escort to the housing unit that I would be residing in.

The Officer came to pick me up and escorted me to B-Block and as soon as I entered the unit I was bombarded by so many familiar faces. But the one that stood out to me the most and the one I thought I'd be less likely to ever see again was my man Rizz. Rizz was from Brooklyn, New York and he and I met back in 1999 at the Garner Correctional Institute in Newtown, Connecticut just before I would be sent to Big Stone Gap, Virginia to do some time at the Wallens Ridge State Prison. Me and the brother hit it off right away after we were introduced by a Correction Officer. The Officer had actually known some of my old friends on the streets and knew that Rizz had spent some time with them while he was on the run in the Virginia Beach, Virginia area. Although I thought I'd never see Rizz again, he had told me that he was back on a violation of his parole and only had about one year to give them before he'd be back off to the life that he had established for himself in Charlotte, North Carolina.

Rizz and two other brothers assisted me with bringing my property to the cell and this brought on some strange looks from the Officers working the unit. I could sense they did not like the attention that I was getting. So, I moved my things into the cell and settled in; however, as I was going through my shit I noticed that my Sean John '*I Am King*' Cologne was missing. This shit had me livid! The one thing I hate with a passion is a motherfucking thief! Moreover, play with someone else's shit and not mine. I had just got into the facility and already shit was looking as if it was about to go downhill for me and really fast.

The next morning, I had gotten up with Rizz and told him about what had taken place with my missing property the night before. I told him that I was sure that it wasn't any of the guys that I knew who were working down in G-Basement. He was then quick to tell me that I should go over to the gym when the Officers called recreation and speak to some of the other guys that were from my town that I had been doing time with since we were all young.

So when recreation was called, I headed out to the gym and while I was walking in the main hallway I ran into this kid from Bridgeport that had a lot of love for brothers from New Haven. When this kid approached he was excited to see that I had made it to a level three, then he went right into telling me all of the people that I knew and hung with in the level four facility. He made sure that he mentioned that I would see my boy Little T and Tat, who were working in the gym. They were both work-out enthusiasts and as soon as I walked through the gym doors there they were hitting the weights hard body. We just greeted each other with the nod of the head and a smile.

I stood and was speaking with these guys and out of the

corner of my eye I could see this Spanish brother who looked very much like the dude that was working in the property room the night before. I turned to Little T and Tat and asked them if the kid I had my eyes on worked in the property room or not? They both stated that the kid in fact worked down there. However, before I could act on what I intended on doing to this piece of shit they posed the question...why? I had let both of them know that I had oil/cologne stolen from me out of my property. They advised me to just leave the situation alone; but, I wasn't willing to be able to do that just yet. This is how I know that trauma is some real shit because this situation brought back my first day at Cheshire Correctional Institute when the Spanish brother tried to tell me I was sitting at his table.

I made a B-line straight at this dude, he saw me coming and my minds' eye was telling me he knew exactly why I was approaching him. I stated flat out to him that my oil was stolen out of my property and I wanted it back or he was going to lose his job because if I didn't have it back in my possession by the next time I saw him we were both going to segregation. Yeah! We were going to shoot the head-up! He broke into some broken bilingual shit like he was oblivious to my blaming him for the shit and started telling me that he would have his boss call me down to the A/P room first thing in the morning because they hadn't thrown out the trash and my oil just may be in the trash. I wanted to punch his head off of his fucking shoulders for insulting my intelligence. Why? Because this is some shit you run on a new jack and I was far from any bodies fucking new jack!

The very next morning at about 7:45am, my cell door popped open and the Officer began to yell at the top of his lungs down the tier that I had to go to the A/P room immediately! I took my time getting up, took that morning piss, washed my hands, brushed my teeth, washed my face and got dressed before exiting my cell to head down to the A/P room. I descended the stairs into

G-Basement and when I bent the corner I was waved over to the room where they had processed my property on Friday night. As I stood in front of the desk with an officer seated behind it, I could see that he had pulled up my information because I could see my photo on the computer screen. This officer went into his spiel about how this Spanish cat was his best worker and if I was missing something he wasn't the one who would've taken it from me. He also knew that I could be a problem and I wasn't to be fucked with after reading my history. He then gave me his word that if he could ever do anything for me I could count on him to handle it for me. Let's just say I held him to his word and he kept it.

Shortly after I returned to my cell the Deputy Warden would make his presence known to me by stopping by my rest. Little did I know it would be someone that was very familiar with me as much as I was with him. He told me that he was the sole reason why I had landed at Osborn to begin with. No other facility wanted me on their open compounds because they were under the impression that this would give me too much range to spread the God Spell (gospel) or teachings of the Nation of Gods and Earths. Moreover, he made it clear to me that I should find something to do with myself while I was there because they would be watching for me to make a mistake of any kind where they could come and remove me from the facility. I told him that it wasn't my determined idea to disturb the normal operations of the facility; but, I would not stand for being mistreated while I was here either!

By the end of the week I would be moved over to the Q's which is the unit (Q-1) inmates were placed in until they got their job assignments. The Q-2 & 3 units were strictly for the clothing factory and officers' clothing and Q4 was the kitchen Block. I requested to be assigned to the kitchen and due to the fact that word was out that I was the official chef in the prison, I got into the kitchen in no time at all. My first job assignment was working the line serving food; however, that didn't last long.

One day while I was working the A-line, the big boss rolled up on me to put a face to the name of the individual everyone was talking about. The head supervisor then went into a series of questions surrounding food service and as quickly as he could spit them out I'd fire back an answer. During this time the facility was baking their bread for one meal a day and purchasing the rest of the bread from a vendor. So, the boss asked me if I thought there was a way I could make bread for two meals instead of one. I told him it was possible; but, he needed to have people working that possessed a passion for baking. He couldn't just have some dudes working that were only working for the $1.25 they were getting for a days' work. He allowed me to keep the guys that were in the position as bakers and show them the science of baking. In a weeks' time we came up with a new schedule and were baking two meals of bread a day and saving the facility about forty-thousand dollars a year in purchases from their vendor. This is just to give light to the impact I have been able to have on any building I may find myself in.

While working in the kitchen, I would talk to my boy Big Mike from Bridgeport and since he always was able to walk away from our talks with a jewel or two he would tell me I should join this group he and some other brothers had been down for some time were a part of. The group was called Changing Criminal Thinking (CCT) group and was run by this ole school addiction services counselor in the facility. Big Mike had ole girl come through and check for me and she invited me down to the hospital basement where the addiction services was located and where they held their weekly meetings. When I went to check out the meeting, I was surprised to see so many familiar faces that I hadn't seen in some time and all of these brothers had over two decades in the system already. Some I did not think would ever consider changing their criminal ways of thinking.

I went through the formalities of introducing myself to individuals who I have known for the twenty-one-years that I had been incarcerated with during this time. These guys embraced me with open arms and knew I had something to offer in the area of change. However, the program would be short lived just several months after my introduction into the group because this light weight, white female counselor who was trusted with overseeing a group of murderers had accepted a transfer to the Hartford County Jail where she could work with individuals coming in off of the streets with a drug addiction. Because the brothers in the group had built a bond we would see each other at chow, the gym and the library and talk about how our lives have been continuously changing as we grow and develop into the men we are supposed to be. We were always wondering what we could do to bring something like this back into existence. For a while we had nothing to fall back on but each other.

### *My thoughts*

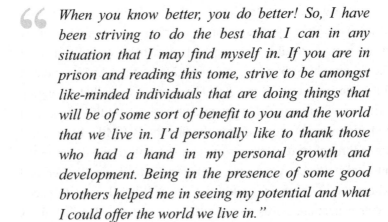 *When you know better, you do better! So, I have been striving to do the best that I can in any situation that I may find myself in. If you are in prison and reading this tome, strive to be amongst like-minded individuals that are doing things that will be of some sort of benefit to you and the world that we live in. I'd personally like to thank those who had a hand in my personal growth and development. Being in the presence of some good brothers helped me in seeing my potential and what I could offer the world we live in."*

# 13

# S.O.S...WORDS, WAYS, & ACTIONS

All of the brothers from the Changing Criminal Thinking Group were still traveling throughout the prison with this positive mental attitude about themselves. However, we became saddened by what we were seeing on a daily basis in the prison and that was recidivism! Brothers were coming back into the prison system at an alarming rate and their excuses were sickening to us because here we were fighting our asses off for the opportunity to get into the world and these ass holes were literally feeding the machine their human flesh.

We were the example for brothers to see when it came to living right in the system. Cats were doing whatever they could to be in our company. We possessed this unique like mindedness about ourselves that stood out amongst everybody and we were given our due respect for such. Several of the brothers from the CCT Group were peer mentors in the drug programs and were having an impact in those programs; however, if you weren't in their block you weren't getting that mental food that they were offering up to assist one in their change.

So, my man T-Nice had an idea about how he could get the Counselor Supervisor to authorize him to bring some dudes down to the hospital basement so he could have a discussion with them about the choices that they were making in their lives. These were some young brothers that were fresh off of the streets and really didn't want to hear what nobody had to say to them because they were already under the impression that they knew it all. That is until T-Nice spoke. This brother spoke with such passion he could easily bring these dudes to tears with the truths he was hitting them with.

The Counselor Supervisor was in earshot of it all and in no time she suggested to T-Nice that he should put together a proposal for that program. Because he had been reading some studies out of some place in Ohio, on the Skills of Socialization, that's what he thought he would title the program. So, T-Nice and Sunny Red approached me to put together the proposal which I drafted immediately for the brothers because I have always been in support of what they were doing. But, T-Nice asked me to come and present what I had wrote to the Counselor Supervisor who didn't know me from a fucking hole in the wall; but, I was down.

I went to work the next morning and sat at the computer so that I could put the finishing touches on my work. I even put a cover page on it to make it look professional and made several copies to hand out to those in attendance during the meeting. It was about noon when the Officer working my unit told me that a Counselor had called the unit and wanted me to go down to the hospital basement for a program. This officer had no idea that I would be presenting a program when I got down there. When I arrived these brothers were all down there waiting for me to show up. T-Nice, Sunny Red, Universal Light, Keese, Little T and Sincere Yakil, all showed me some love when I entered the small room where we were to meet with the Counselor Supervisor. I was there all of ten minutes when in walked this use-to-be fat chick who looked at me like I had three fucking heads then looked to T-Nice and asked him "who's this and what's he doing here?" One thing I love about my brother Nice Is that he gets a kick out of checking these people whenever they get out of pocket. T-Nice looked at her like he was a pimp and she was one of his hoes and told her directly 'this is Ray, and he's with us!' not another word came out of her mouth; so, I took it to mean she knew her place and was prepared to stay in it.

I gave my spiel on what we were proposing and she accepted it. However, she made several suggestions for changes to be made before she could take it to her bosses.

We all adhered to the changes and didn't see a problem with what she was suggesting. The following week we put out sign-up sheets for the housing units so we could start running groups and from that day on the Skills of Socialization Program was off to the races.

During this time, Sincere and I were given approval and access to use two computers in the school where we were able to create the draft of what would become our curriculum as well as the biographies of the founding members of the Skills of Socialization program. We were also assigned counselor Rexach to act as a liaison between S.O.S. and the administration. Once this was done, we all went over the roles that we would play in executing each session to the participants of the group. My role was to take the minutes and leave the group with an impact statement that would send them back to their cells thinking about some serious thought provoking shit! Because I was dealing with the science of living mathematics the brothers knew that I could be counted on to deliver some powerful shit to make these young brothers question why they ever entered into a life of crime to begin with.

Sunny Red had attended a job fair being held in the library one week and just so happened to run into an old face from the neighborhood. This person (Holly Wasilewski) that he ran into was a retired New Haven Police Officer and now the Reentry and Community Outreach Coordinator for the United States' Attorney's Office for the District of Connecticut. Red put her on to what we were doing and invited her to our weekly investors meeting that we had every Friday in the Chapel. Dr. Rev. Williams, had become a supporter of ours and was all in when it came to allowing us to use the chapel for the meetings. Each week's meeting would link us with someone on the outside that was willing to link us with someone else that was willing to assist us in the furtherance of our agenda. I mean every fucking staff member in the building was shouting S.O.S. and wanting their hands in on what we had going on. The program even had these counselors hating on each other for a spot on our team. When the picks were made as to which counselors we wanted to work with, we began to see the other sides of those that were dying to get in on the ride that we were about to take the Department of Correction on.

For several months our groups were being held in the hospital basement; however, we began to run into some problems with the addiction services counselors. Word was getting around that they didn't want us running the program in the hospital basement anymore because they had seen that we had more inmates volunteering to take part in our program then they were willing to go to the programs that were mandatory in order for them to get out of prison. This also scared the shit out of the counselors where we were being seen as a threat because they started talking about we were going to take their fucking jobs.

During this time Ms. Dianne Jones from the City of Hartford had attended a Friday meeting and we expressed to her that we would like to get all of the Mayors from our major cities to the table with us to address some of the issues of reentry. She jumped at the opportunity to get Mayor Luke Bronin to have a sit down with us. Two weeks later we were giving a presentation for the Hartford City Mayor and he pulled no punches when it came to meeting us. He brought in a press team along with the Hartford Courant newspaper. On October 1, 2016 the very next day after the meeting there we were with our faces plastered in between the pages of the Hartford Courant *"BREAKING DOWN WALLS"* in Connecticut it's the inmates leading in counseling... Once this hit the paper, these fucking counselors lost their god damn minds and swore that the administration at any minute would be walking them all out of the building and biding them all farewell!

Seeing the animosity that we were causing in the basement, T-Nice and some of the other guys went over to the chapel and approached Rev. Williams about us being able to use the chapel to run the program. Being the spiritual man that Rev. Williams is, he could not fathom why grown fucking adults were fearing the act of a few good men. Listen, it has always been said that the motherfuckers closest to the problem, are the one closest to the solution! Those hating ass counselors never had what it took to get into the minds and hearts of these men and help them see their life had meaning, purpose and that they were so much more than what the system had labeled them as. We were them, they were us and we exploited this commonality by speaking to the heart of their plight. We had Unit managers coming to our meetings and thanking us for stopping some of the incidents that were taking place in their units. They were telling us that whenever two or more inmates were about to get into something, there were always other inmates who would be reminding each other about the comradery that was being built in the S.O.S. Program.

We were connecting with brothers who we did time with who were out in the community doing good and invited these brothers back into the cages that once held them so that they could deliver their personal message to those who wanted to take part in the speaking engagements we were giving. Our speaking engagements were open to the entire facility; but, the Shift commanders would only allow us to have a maximum of one hundred and fifty people in attendance. We had brothers like Daee McKnight, Imam Lyle Hasan Jones, Fred X. Hodges, William Outlaw, Daryl McGraw, Alex Ketchum, Gerald Scott, Louis Reed, Dan Varley, and our main man Juan Castillo from 94.3 WYBC. I'm actually listening to the best varieties of hits and oldies as I write this book. Also, we had the Dwayne Betts an ex-offender with a law degree from Yale, Randel Horton an ex-offender who's now an English Professor at the University of New Haven, Prof. William Jelani Cobbs, Prof. James Forman, Michael Chochos an ex-offender with a Master's degree from Yale School of Seminary, Katherine Boudin an ex-offender who's now a Professor at Columbia University, State Representative Brandon McGee, Toni Harp the Mayor for the City New Haven, Author and Motivational Speaker LaShawn "Lala" Middleton drove all the way from Charlotte, North Carolina to give us some of her jewels and motivation. This sister was fine as all hell, mentally and physically. However, nothing excites me more than an intelligent black woman who in her vulnerability was willing to share her world with a room full of men who spent some time taking advantage of women at some point or another in their own lives.

In no time at all we were pulling in supporters from near and far. Holly had brought so many people on broad to assist us along our mission to reduce recidivism. We had the support of people like Brent Peterkin who is the Statewide Coordinator for Project Longevity; Assistant Attorney U.S. Vanessa Avery; New York 2$^{nd}$ Circuit Court of Appeals Judge John Walker and his daughter Katharine; and a host of other Federal Judges and Prosecutors. On April 27, 2017 we were even awarded by United States' Attorney Deirdre Daly and the United States Department of Justice for the work that we were doing. We were getting recognition from our local news outlets and stories were being run in Newspapers all throughout the country. There was even a story on yahoo news out in the UK. This was big for seven guys who came to prison when they were juveniles and we went from having our names in the papers for the crimes that we had committed to reading about ourselves in a new light for the lives that we were saving.

We knew that the Skills of Socialization program was put together to address some of the ills that the younger generation was facing with criminality in their communities. So, we had an idea to see if the Administration would allow us to go over to MYI and speak with their population. It was even thought to film this trip as a documentary from the time we woke up in the morning brushing our teeth and washing our faces through the rest of the day. The Warden and Deputy Warden from the Manson Youth Institute were impressed with this idea of ours; however, we could not go back into MYI because it was a state law that forbids one from being over the age of twenty-two and returning to the facility. Their only option was to send ten youth from MYI up to Osborn Correctional Institute so they could be involved in the program. Within a weeks' time we received the first group of participants and twelve weeks later they had completed the program without any problems and the young fellas were telling the staff back at the facility that they liked the program so much that they didn't want to stop going.

I can still remember the speech I gave at their graduation from the program.

*Good afternoon!*

*First, I'd like to thank the staff who saw our vision and gave their all in seeing it to fruition. The Wardens, those at Central Office, Rev. Williams, Counselor Rexach and lastly the Correction Officers entrusted to safely transport these young men from the Manson Youth Institute so that they may take part in the Skills of Socialization Program.*

*Having committed our crimes at an age much younger than the young men that we are honoring here today--- we all have shared in the idea of being able to get the S.O.S. program into MYI, to work with our young brothers who; as we once had, suffered from behavioral problems, be it, poor attitude, low self-esteem, peer pressure, etc.*

*Although the powers that be have brought MYI to us, we*

have not given up on getting into MYI; because, we know that there are hundreds of other lives hanging in the balance as that van departs on Thursdays.

I want to commend the graduates of S.O.S. for wanting to take part in the program. It truly says a lot about you, that you would be willing to wake up and go through what you had to endure to get here each week...some cold mornings but you guys endured so that you would have the ability to come directly in contact with some different information as Tino would say.

You guys have decided for yourselves that it's time to seek something other than what you already knew, because your old ways of thinking weren't leading you anywhere... that's street smarts! You guys have gone from being schooled about the streets to being schooled in a new way.

When we enroll into a school, it requires us to become educated or if not the school would be failing its students. Correct? Well, just as S.O.S. has not failed you these past weeks, we hold dear to the notion of no child left behind when it comes to a commitment to reducing recidivism amongst our youth.

This education that you have received from the facilitators of S.O.S. qualifies you to be productive. It qualifies you to elevate the way you think, civilize the way you act and improve the way you feel about yourself in order for you to do what's best for you and society as a whole!

You guys still have time to continue to work on yourselves and this road is not an easy one I can assure you; because, none of us got it overnight.

So, let me leave you with this;" Ephesians 6:12 - For we wrestle not against flesh and blood, but against principalities, against powers, against the rulers of the darkness of this world, against spiritual wickedness in high places...high places! Your minds are these high places and your mindset is everything and you are what you think!

So, continue to think right thoughts because as I shared with *you in the past, your thoughts become words, your words become actions, your actions become habits and your habits become your character. Peace!*

This shit was bugging us out and bringing smiles to all of our faces at the same time. We were seeing the fruits of our labor and making some good accomplishments. Just the mere thought of our families seeing us in the papers for doing some good shit was so fucking exciting! We were making our own personal mark on the world. However, just as things were getting good the system would find a way to fuck up a good thing.

Guys who attended our group were going to parole and presenting themselves in a way that the parole board hadn't seen before and these guys were attributing their conduct to what they had learned in the group. We were getting guys parole and just so happened that one day during our Friday meeting one of the big wigs dropped in unannounced to see if we were some real brothers qualified to teach the shit we were teaching. I'll just say that Ms. Patricia Thomas-Camp left the meeting in awe and impressed at how professional we were when operating under Robert's Rule of Order! It is said that the first impression is the best impression. Well, let's just say that our first impression was the only impression we had to give.

Unbeknownst to us, the Skills of Socialization Program wasn't just making a lot of fucking noise in the building, we were on the radar of the Commissioner and the talk amongst those up at the DOC headquarters. Many, if not all of the higher ups knew exactly who each and every one of the founding members of Skills of Socialization Program were and they could not really believe that we were moving with so much energy, strength and power towards doing the right thing. Especially when their last dealings with us was probably when they were putting our asses in segregation for some foul shit we did in their facility. The one thing they did not know; but, was sure to soon find out was that they were no longer dealing with the immature

Juveniles that the criminal justice system threw away as incorrigible but the grown men that we have become even in the midst of this physical hell.

On December 18, 2017 they would start their investigation and came down on several members of the group that were responsible for building the curriculum, meaning those who had computer access. I and two other brothers were placed in segregation for sixteen days pending investigation. Our computers were removed from our work areas and sent up to the intelligence unit to be looked over by their IT specialist. Upon completion of their investigation it had been determined that no violations had taken place on our part. However, as disappointed as they were they had to save face; so, they held us in segregation pending transfer. On January 3, 2018 I was transferred to Cheshire Correctional Institute.

### *My thoughts*

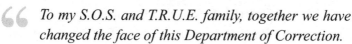 *To my S.O.S. and T.R.U.E. family, together we have changed the face of this Department of Correction.*

*I know that there are those who would like to keep their focus on reimagining prison; however, we work day in and day out to deconstruct the very walls that have been designed to hold us. Continue to do what you were destined to do and together we can change the world!"*

# 14

# MENTORING

I arrived at the Cheshire Correctional Institute on January 3, 2018 and on this day I had to experience something that I had never experienced before in all of my time incarcerated. I went through the intake process when I got to the facility and was taken through all of the dehumanizing shit that comes along with entering a new facility. The strip search, grab your balls, bend over spread your ass cheeks; yeah all that shit! I was removed from the bullpen and escorted by a Correction Officer to the housing unit that I was assigned to. Upon my arrival into the unit I could see several officers going through someone's property and checking things off on the property matrix form. It was clear to me that several individuals had gone to segregation for breaking a rule in the facility. I took about ten steps further into South Block Five as the officer who brought me there passed off my identification card to the Correctional Officer working the block. The Officer told me that I was in cell number 527, and she then proceeded to pop open the door. As I descended the stairs, someone yelled out from behind their cell door "I don't think you want to go in that cell bro!" Then the door swung wide open and I could see a head peek out. The head that I saw was very familiar to me from the Osborn Correctional Institute. It was this young white kid that was a known homosexual who was transferred out of Osborn to Cheshire; because, he had gotten caught for allegedly letting some guys run a train on him.

I have vowed to never allow myself to be put in a living situation where I would share a cell with a homosexual. I don't have anything against those who chose to live this way of life; however, I'm just not living around it! When I saw this kid, I spoke with the female officer working the block and expressed to her that she should call the lieutenant and ask if I could move into one of the other empty cells in the unit. This chick looked over at me and flat out told me that if I wasn't going into the cell they had assigned me to, I was going to segregation! I peered back over at this bitch, matched her stare and told her that it would now be best she called the lieutenant because I was going to the box. So in just five minutes into my being in the block, I would now be turning around and heading in a total opposite direction. My only other option was to refuse housing and go off to segregation.

So, she called the lieutenant and they sent an officer back up to the housing unit to escort me back down to the A/P room where they locked my ass up in a bullpen alone until about 3:00am. Mind you, I had gotten into the facility at around 9:30pm. They didn't know but these motherfuckers were playing a psychological game I was well conditioned for. So, I just sat on my ass and patiently waited for them to come for me. My only request to the lieutenant was that they issue my disciplinary report before the morning so I could cop out to the infraction. The very next morning I pled guilty to a class A ticket for refusing housing and was given seven days in segregation. After I pled out on the ticket, the Disciplinary Officer sat back in his chair and told me flat out I would never have to worry about having to go through this again as if some kind of note would be

selves but we learned a lot about ourselves in this setting. This would lead to us becoming peer mentors in a lot of the Offender Accountability Programs like Anger Management, Good Intentions Bad Choices, Embracing Fatherhood, Voices. All of these programs were put in place by the Department of Correction and mandated to assist its sentenced population towards their rehabilitation before they enter back into society. If such mandatory programming is not completed upon an inmates' parole hearing date, one could seriously run the risk of not making parole or having their parole date rescheduled predicated upon completion of whichever programs that they need to finish.

The Cheshire Mentors Group was responsible for many other things in the institution and was operating in subcommittees to accomplish their goals. When I had entered the Mentors Group another mentor; Carl Alexander, whom I was pretty cool with had spoken with me at length over several weeks about an idea he had with regards to adding on another subcommittee to the mentors Group and he wanted me to take part in it. His idea was to start what would later become the Criminal Justice Committee (CJC). The committee members would consist of myself, Marco Camacho, Gary Garner, Jamal Burke, Michael Cox, Levern Grant, Jamal Jenkins and Floyd X. Simms.

The Mission of CJC was: Re-Balancing the Scales of Justice & Breaking the chains of Mass Incarceration. The Goals & Purpose was: To create a progressive dialogue platform sparking criminal justice reform on a state & federal level. Our goal is to foster awareness amongst legislators, policymakers, legal organizations & law students, that promote & maintain public safety and effect changes to juvenile justice, sentencing policies, policing practices,and the over-criminalization process.

At first a lot of the other mentors did not want to see his vision or just didn't want to be a part of anything this brother was about for their own personal reasons. Look I get it, we all have some strong personalities and a lot of times they don't mesh quite the way we would like them to; but, that should never stop us from working towards one common goal. Our ultimate goal should always be our freedom and our individual personalities should never come in between us working together to get home.

I was voted in as the Chair of the Criminal Justice Committee and we went right to work to capture the attention of those who we felt we needed to get in contact with. We became responsible for the tours in the facility that dealt with college professors and their students coming in. We would give them a presentation that would start with a formal introduction from each member. My intro would go something like "Hello, my name is Ray Boyd. I'm from the City of New Haven, in 1989 at the age of seventeen I committed a murder and I have been incarcerated for twenty-eight and a half years. Once everyone went through stating their names, their crimes and how long they have been incarcerated, we would tell them what an average day looks like behind these walls and then we would entertain a series of questions related to prison and our lives before incarceration and while we are serving out our time. We would be asked some of the most common questions that are usually asked like; 'What made you commit your crime?' 'Did you fear that you'd get raped coming to prison?' 'Do you have children?' 'What is the food like in prison?' 'How hard is it for you while doing your time?' 'Do you fear that you'll die before you get out?' 'Have you ever seen anyone get stabbed?' 'What do you miss the most?' Whenever we would give our responses, they would become so at awe at how articulate we were when they left our presence we would always hear about how much these professors and students enjoyed interacting with us and how this has reshaped the ways in which they have been conditioned to view prisoners. Many of them have even chosen to change their field of study to major in criminal justice or an introduction to correction.

The Criminal Justice Committee had taken on a life of its

own and outside of the invites that we were sending out we were receiving a lot of requests from government and state agencies to meet with us. States' Attorneys and heads of the Juvenile Probation Department wanted to meet with us and I am sure that these engagements would provide those who don't really get to see us other than from behind the defense table a different perspective on the lives of the men who have taken their rehabilitation seriously.

In several months' time the Criminal Justice Committee was disbanded by the powers that be and never fully explained to the committee members what warranted the disbandment. Personally I would say that it was due to the fact that there was another program that existed in the facility at this time that the entire Department of Correction was invested in and they could not afford to see this program overshadowed by the Criminal Justice Committee. I could assure you that had CJC stayed in existence, the committee would have served some good for violent offenders that are being overlooked by those who are looking to reimagine prison and refusing to include violent offenders.

The program was a model of prison reform that former Governor Dan Malloy, former Correction Commissioner Scott Semple and the VERA Institute of Justice had traveled to Germany to see and upon their return they went to work figuring out how to implement a version of what they had experienced and what would be the designated location for the program. Cheshire Correctional Institution would become the location because it was centrally located where the families of those chosen to take a part in the program would be able to visit their loved ones. Former Warden Scott Erfe, had thought it best to use creditable lifers as mentors for this program and had convinced the Commissioner of this. The Mentors were to be chosen from the Mentors (Lifers) Group. Ten in total and they would all be given single cells where they were to live and work amongst the mentees in a twenty-four hour setting. These ten brothers would put their minds together and birth what would become the T.R.U.E. program. T.R.U.E. stands for Truthfulness, Respectfulness, Understanding and Elevating. They even came up with a pledge that went

*"The T.R.U.E. Program is our stepping stone into manhood, **T**ruthfulness to one self and others, **R**espectfulness toward the community, **U**nderstanding ourselves and what brought us here, and **E**levating into success."*

The model of the T.R.U.E. Program by Warden Erfes' design of using the lifers as mentors had proven to be the ultimate success. So much so that the program was awarded by the National Institute of Corrections as the safest unit on all levels, i.e., Federal, State, and local. Just eighteen months into the inception of the program, the idea was being floated around to start a reentry portion of the T.R.U.E. Program. Therefore, they would be in search of some new prospects from the mentors group to kick this thing off. However, because I had just gotten to the facility and into the mentors group, I figured that I didn't stand much of a chance amongst those who stood before me as far as being selected as one who would have qualified to develop what this Reentry portion of the program would look like. There were roughly thirty or so individuals that were a part of the mentors group before I even came in. The one thing that I was sure of was that when I went up for the interview, I would give all within my power to secure a place in this new unit. On October 1, of 2018 one of the lieutenants who did my interview; with several other staff and mentors, delivered my letter of acceptance to become a mentor in the T.R.U.E. program where I would work to develop T.R.U.E. Reentry.

Not only had the T.R.U.E. Program received national attention, the program was about to blow the fuck up and receive national recognition! The Television News Magazine - 60 Minutes - was filming a segment of their show titled '***The Rock***" and would be about an aspiring Collegiate basketball player

Shyquin Dix, who had left the T.R.U.E. program (prison) to play basketball at the University of Maine Presque Isle. So, Shyquin had literally found himself on the prison-to-college pipeline. This segment was scheduled to air on March 30, 2019 during the NCAA College Basketball Tournament.

My family and friends who knew that I was in the program helping these emerging adults were getting at me and telling me about how they all were seeing glimpses of me whenever the trailer would run about the show and how they couldn't wait until it aired. When the show eventually aired, the very next day a lot of the staff members were feeling some kind of way about how the story had highlighted the relevance of what it meant to have the mentors in such a setting and how effective our presence was. This is not to say that the officers did not have a hand in the laurels of the unit but the main focus was on Shyquin Dix and how his mentor played a role in assisting him with overcoming the obstacles or norms associated with prison life, not what the day in a life of the Correctional Officers looked like. I'm sure that every news station in the country has footage of that in their archives.

I had the pleasure of working with ten men to develop the T.R.U.E. reentry program which is a ten-point syllabus that is geared towards helping the mentee make a smooth transition back into the community as a returning citizen. So far the mentees who have left the T.R.U.E. reentry program has yet to return to prison. On February 4, 2019 I toured Connecticut State Governor Ned Lamont and newly appointed Department of Correction Commissioner Rollin Cook in the program and it was an amazing opportunity.

Things were going as best they could for the most part before the Covid-19 Pandemic came along and put things on lockdown. Since this time, I have continued to mentor in the capacity that the institution will allow me to.

### *My thoughts*

 *The Covid-19 Virus came into everybody's world and put a halt on everything. I know that it personally affected my life in a lot of ways, some good and some bad. Because of my medical condition, I sought release on medical parole because if I were to contract Covid-19, it could prove to be fatal. My request was denied. This was followed up by a request to be released on an Appeal bond while I waited for the outcome of my appeal that was before the appellate court. This too was denied! Prior to the pandemic I had filed for a sentence modification with the Prosecutor of the New Haven Superior Court and due to the pandemic the prosecutor had agreed to allow me to have a hearing on the modification; but, would not agree to a reduction in time. In June of 2020, this request for a sentence modification was denied. However, throughout it all I have continued to remain steadfast on keeping a positive mental attitude while serving out the remainder of my time. Also, my focus has not been affected when it comes to me being a mentor to the young men that I have built some beautiful relationships with."*

# 15

# FIND YOUR LANE... AND STAY IN IT

I have found my lane and I intend on staying on this straight path for the rest of my life. I look forward to becoming deeply involved in the criminal justice system as an advocate against a lot of the injustices that I have seen firsthand and know continues to take place; but, is overlooked by those who refuse to see wrong in the normalities of the system. I aspire to one day go to college and study law so that I can help those that I will be leaving behind when I am released in the very near future.

Thank you for reading this body of work and I ask that you continue to check for me because I will not be far away.

### *My thoughts*

 *I look forward to my impending release date to come soon so that I can enter back into Society and become an asset to my family and my community. I look forward to establishing a stronger relationship with my son Ray! I look forward to building a loving home with my wife Jackie and being a father*

*figure to Chloe. I look forward to going on family
walks with Chloe and her dog Blush."*

*"I cannot wait to hug my mother and tell her
just how much I love her for loving me 100% for all
of the rights and wrongs that I have done in my life!
I love you mom !!!"*

I would just like to inform my readers that on December 2, 2020 I fell ill from Covid-19 and had to spend over a week in the hospital in critical condition; however, I am recovering well. That was the bad news...the good news is that on July 13, 2021 I had a sentence modification hearing. On July 14th, the judge granted the motion, which means that I will be released by the end of November 2021! If you enjoyed this book, or if you didn't, I would like to invite you to share your thoughts with me at info@rasunallah.com

# SHOUT OUTS

A crazy shout out goes to my brothers in that free cipher that have continued to show me love upon your return home and throughout this journey: Kieyshon 'Non-G.' Taylor, the Visualizer-it is because of your God consciousness that you are sought out to provide others with some insight into their futures so continue on being a beacon of light; Kyle '*K.B.*' Baines, my brother-niggas talking about how hard society is; but, coming home after two plus decades in the can you make the shit look easy. Nyle, will be proud to have you as his father; Tyquan Bailey; Mike Capelas I want to thank you for holding me down; Gregg '*NYG*' Booker, Harlem is a much better place with you home. Yeah! The streets still go east to west and the Avenues still go north to south. Levern 'V-Zoc' Grant 31 years of your life you gave to this system-Live Free! Maceo Streater continue to do good things and be a support for the brothers on the inside. Edward "Brooklyn Boo" Andrews of SCRIP; Darryl 'Head' Douglas; Jewu Richardson; James Jeter; Hon. Floyd X. Simms; Shelton Adams; William 'Joey' Brown, my brother I want to thank you for always being there for me and imparting your wisdom whenever I sought you out for it.

Shawn "Goodie" Crocker, Darryl "D.V." Valentine, Thomas "Tom-Tom" Lane. Robert Jeffrey, Portsmouth, Virginia is blessed to have a stand up brother like yourself to represent P-Town...even though you're a GLOBAL nigga at heart!

Brent Peterkin, Statewide Coordinator for Project Longevity; Holly Wasilewski, Reentry & Community Outreach Coordinator for the U.S. Attorney's Office District of CT; William "June Boy" Outlaw, Connecticut Violence Intervention Program; Fred X. Hodges, and Daee' McKnight, Mr. Michael Bambino for believing in the men of S.O.S. and having the willingness to see past our past transgressions and work with us to better the community at large.

I would like to give a shout out to the Nation of Gods and Earths. Especially the Gods who have been my A-alike and companions in my growth and development into the knowledge of myself. Born Self Allah; Prince Supernatural Allah; Precise Unique Master Allah (R.I.P.); Divine Allah,

Supreme Darkness Allah; Supreme Trilogy Allah; Meek Sincere Allah; Saij Allah; Eye Beyond Allah; My companion Prince U'neek Majestic Allah; S.A.G.E. (Da'Culture Seed); Carmi 'Hiram' Kellman (R.I.P.); Barkim Allah; Prince Medina Allah; Asiatic Mustbe Mathematics Allah; True Allah; I-Tru; Manifest Allah; to all the Gods that reached into this interior cipher to add-on during my mental wisdom Allah rule to cee Allah World Manifest; my enlightener Allah Blackness-all praise is due to you God for entrusting that when you gave me the knowledge of myself as the Father gave it to his Suns I would never drop the torch!

To my brothers in the struggle Kevin Stanley; Edgar Tatum; Albert Stephens; Mark Ambrose; David Gibbs; Jamal Jenkins; Carl Alexander; Jermaine Young; Douglas Davis; Eric Ham; Shelton Adams; Troy Westberry; John Moye; Clyde Meikle; John Pittman; Andrew Dickson; Gilfredo Santiago; Michael Bernier; Eric Morelli; Davon Eldemire; Taicuan Digsby, my brother-thanks for taking the time out of your days to sit and read this body of work and giving me some feedback…your thoughts truly mattered to me!

A big shout out to my niece Natalie for her entrepreneurial endeavor over at *ModernandHippie.com* and my sister Janet for doing her thing with *HillRosebyJb.com*. Listen, it is important that as blacks in America we begin to put our energy and time into wealth building, saving, investing and entrepreneurship. Alyssa, I haven't forgotten you and what you are doing with *Flawlysaccessories.com*. I wish you all the best in your individual successes.

A special shout out and thank you to Attorney Alexander T. Taubes for your unwavering support. You are destined to be the top lawyer in this State in the years to come. I know that I will always come to you before seeking the counsel of any other Attorney!

Connecticut State Senator Gary Holder-Winfield (10th District), you have no idea what your support in filing the Amicus Brief means to myself and so many others.

The U.S. of A.
The Urban Soldiers of America, Hold your heads…

Made in the USA
Middletown, DE
14 December 2021

53943859R00076